The Path the Ball Takes

Clayton Johnson

New Harbor Press
RAPID CITY, SD

Copyright © 2025 by Clayton Johnson.

All rights reserved. No part of this publication may be reproduced, distributed or transmitted in any form or by any means, including photocopying, recording, or other electronic or mechanical methods, without the prior written permission of the publisher, except in the case of brief quotations embodied in critical reviews and certain other noncommercial uses permitted by copyright law. For permission requests, write to the publisher, addressed "Attention: Permissions Coordinator," at the address below.

Johnson/New Harbor Press
1601 Mt. Rushmore Rd, Ste 3288
Rapid City, SD 57701
www.NewHarborPress.com

Ordering Information:
Quantity sales. Special discounts are available on quantity purchases by corporations, associations, and others. For details, contact the "Special Sales Department" at the address above.

The Path the Ball Takes/Clayton Johnson. —1st ed.
ISBN 978-1-63357-465-6

Contents

Track Star 1
That's who us Joseph's are 7
Driveway Therapy Sessions 13
Back To School 17
Seasons Change 23
Try Outs 31
Team Bonding 37
Group Hang 43
First Game 51
Reconciliation 63
Shooters Shoot 69
A Place to Fit In 75
(Interlude) Wyatt's Story 81
2nd Game 89
After Party 95
Winter Break 99

Most Valuable Lesson 103
What We Find in the Flames 107
Christmas 111
Letting Go 115
Playoff's 119
Banquet 131
  ALMOST FIVE YEARS LATER: 135

CHAPTER ONE

Track Star

"Next up we have Rick Joseph! A high jumper from West Des Moines High School that is making waves here in his sophomore campaign." I hear the announcer call my name as I step up to the line. The butterflies in my belly start flapping their wings as I hear the crowd in the stands start to get fired up. I try to calm myself by zoning everything out and just looking down at my white and brown track shoes. It never seems to work though.

"We all are expecting big things from Rick here today at this district championships event. After all, he did shock us all last year by taking 2nd place in this event only as a freshman in the Iowa state championships. Losing out only to senior Zain Less, who is now jumping for the University of Iowa. Hopes are high that Rick will be west Des Moines first 3-time state champ! If he clears this bar here and now, he walks away with another district title to match his one from last year!"

The bar is right at 5'10 right now. Needless to say, that's a high jump. I have hit this kind of height one time before when I was getting extra reps in after practice. However, there wasn't hundreds of people with their eyes locked in on me, it was just me and my dad.

I look over to the stands, scanning until I can find him. After a while, I finally do. He's standing on his feet with his arms already in the cheering position in anticipation of what I'm about to do. Wearing a white t-shirt with a big brown STAGS written on the chest. The Stag is our school's mascot. There's a lot of deer in Iowa so it always seemed fitting to me.

My dad is of course sitting next to my mom, Violet. Next to her, my best friend in the world, Wyatt Herbert, along with his own better half Ava Fong. It was nice of them to come and support.

Me and my dad lock eyes, and he gives me a wink like 'You got this son.' and just like that I can feel the nerves that are making my arms feel like they weigh as much as truck calm down a bit. I take a big breath in... 'Alright,' I think to myself 'never mind how many people are out there, Rick... you're not going to let your dad down.

After two quick breaths I start making strides toward the bar. Left after right, left after right, making the height the bar is set at only seem taller with every step closer to it I get. Soon it's so close it's just out of reach. I put my legs under me and push off the earth so hard it's like I'm trying to knock out of orbit. Now off the ground, I arch my back and let my head pass just over the bar and my body follows suit. I land on the nice pad below me and quickly I stand up in disbelief and throw my arms in the air having made the jump!

Relief fills my heart. I think 'What am I acting so shocked for? I said it myself that I wasn't going to let my dad down.' I peer back up into the stands to see my dad and Wyatt losing their minds and hugging with their girls promptly giggling at them beside them.

After I get changed and congratulate other members of my team that are also moving on to state in their events, I walk out to meet my ever so adoring fans in the parking lot outside the stadium.

I walk up to the group and my dad quickly grabs hold of me and hugs me with enough force to break a rib. "That's my boy!

I knew you could do it! A leaping Stag if I ever saw one!" he exclaims.

"Paul, let him go. You're embarrassing him in front of his friends." my mother responds with. Wyatt then lifts an arm for a high five with a "WAY TO GO MAN!" attached to it. Followed up by a "Great job out there, Rick!" from Ava.

"Come on kids." my dad says. "Victory chocolate shakes on me tonight. Rick don't worry, we're going to burn them off practicing for state tomorrow." Wyatts face lights up at the idea of free shakes and he says "Mr. Joseph, you're the dad I never had."

Wyatt has a dad. An involved one, at that. I guess his loyalty must just lay at the bottom of a tub of ice cream.

Walking to the car I can't help but think 'What more could a guy really ask for other than good family and friends?' However, shortly after, a second thought pops into my head 'Is the world bigger than just Iowa?'

Sure, it's great here, don't get me wrong. It's just that... well a big part of why me and my dad bond over track so much is because he was an accomplished jumper himself in school. Long jumper, actually. That and hurdles. I have looked at his old numbers from back in the day and the man should have had no problem getting into a big school and getting out there to see the world during his track career. However, he met my mom his senior year and that was that.

No big schools. No competing around the world, or even the country for that matter. He never left Iowa. Which lead to him having me so, I mean, I am not complaining. He seems to have a fulfilling life... it is just not the life I see for myself. It's a big world out there and I want to see it all.

We pull into the parking lot of our local ice cream shop and the big neon sign that reads SCOTTYS SCOOPS lights our path. As we walk inside, the sun is starting to go down. "Get what you want, kids." my mom ensures us as we get to the counter. "One large chocolate! Oh, and throw some peanut butter in there!" Wyatt orders.

"Wyatt, are you forgetting something?" Ava asks, gesturing towards my parents. After a second Wyatt gets the hint and says "Oh right, ha-ha. Thank you, Mr. and Mrs. Joseph."

Ava seconds his thank you to my parents then goes to order "I will have a strawberry shake, please."

I come in right behind her "I'll have one shake made with mint chocolate chip, please."

"Coming right up." the man behind the counter tells us. I look to see my friends with confused looks on their faces. "A mint chocolate chip shake dude?" Wyatt says shaking his head. "You're such an odd ball. If you weren't so athletic, I would say you have no hope of ever getting a girlfriend."

"Oh, so I guess your taste in ice cream is what Ava sees in you? Glad we finally figured that out." I tell him, jokingly.

"No, actually I believe it was my boyish charm." he responds. Ava interjects saying "Yeah, something like that." while lightly punching him in the arm.

They're good together. At first, I worried she would come between me and my friend getting to have guy time but she's actually a welcome addition to the gang. I'll admit, Wyatt must have some sort of charm because if you ask me, Ava is out of his league. Don't get me wrong now, Wyatt is a good-looking guy, and as his best friend I dare say any girl would be lucky to have him.

He has curly brown hair and green eyes. Not overly tall, around 5'10, 2 inches taller than me. Normally dressed like a skater in baggy clothes. Like I said, he's not a bad looking guy, but Ava... she's beautiful. I am saying that objectively. I promise I don't have a thing for her. When I say beautiful, I mean it in every sense of the word. Not just looks. I don't know if I can say I have met a kinder person. The way she puts up with me and Wyatt goofing off makes her fun to be around. Seeing those two together, I can say if I have to lose the position of Wyatts best friend to anyone, I am glad it's her.

She's Thai American with pink highlights in her black hair. She's about 5'4 and when she's not wearing Wyatts hoodies, she almost dresses like she's on her way to a casual business meeting.

We drink our shakes and head home for the night. My mom and dad drop off my friends at their houses. When we pull into my house, my dad asks my mom to give us a minute. She does so and walks inside. My dad turns to me and puts his hand on my shoulder "You looked nervous before that jump today.".

"Yeah, that's because I was." I tell him the truth.

"I know... You know how I know?" he asks.

"How?"

"Because I was you once."

"Yeah, I am sure you we're nervous all the time before you jumped." I say sarcastically. For as long as I have known him, my dad has been a confident man, so thinking about him being scared about something doesn't seem realistic to me. "Do you think all the greats are never scared? Some of them, maybe are not, but for the rest of us we become great when we overcome our fears. Next time you're scared to jump, just remember that's who us Joseph's are, people who overcome."

"Well, dad, that was equal part cheesy and helpful... Thank you." I tell him. He smiles at me and says "Alright, get in there and get some well-earned rest. I love you, son."

"Love you too, dad." I say and I am off to bed.

I get some good sleep. Then, I wake up, go to school, train, rinse and repeat six times, and then before I know it, it's the day to take off to head to the state tournament. If I thought this week dragged on, having to sit through school today was way worse. The anticipation is killing me.

I win this thing and I am one step closer to jumping my way out of this town. Half way though the school day, I get a text from my dad that reads 'Wait for me before you get on the bus, me and mom got you something.' wonder what that could be.

As the end of the day is nearing, Wyatt comes up to me "Hey man how you feeling?".

"I feel ready." I tell him.

"You look ready. I know how hard you've worked all year. The gold is as good as yours."

"Thanks, man. You're coming up to watch right?"

"Am I coming to watch? Brother, I am going to find a way to put that gold medal on you myself."

We share a bro hug and I start walking my way to the bus. A few of the other guys are already on board. We don't leave until 3:30 so we still have a little time. I sit and wait, watching for my dad's car to pull in. I sit and watch until 3:29 and the bus driver stands up to start doing roll call. I give him my best plead to wait just a little longer and tell him my dad will be here to see me off any second now.

Just when I think the driver is about to take off and not wait any longer, I see my mom's car pull in. They must have ridden together. I set out of the bus to claim my gift, whatever it is. I can only hope it's a new pair of cleats. As she parks, I see that, strangely enough, she's alone.

And the closer I get to her my stomach sinks as I can see her mascara running down her red face. She appears to be in a great amount of distress. She stagers toward me and I run to her.

"MOM! What's wrong? Where's dad?" I say, trying not to assume anything, as my mind can sometimes jump to the worst. She hugs me struggling to get out any words out. "Rick." she says bawling, "There's been an accident.".

CHAPTER 2

That's who us Joseph's are

The traffic light camera caught the whole thing. I didn't watch it; mom wouldn't have allowed that. Even if she would have let me see, I don't think I could handle seeing it.

Apparently, he was at a stop light coming from the west. On the south side of the light was a woman in her 30's crossing the street with her 5-year-old little girl. The walk light was on so they should have been all clear. Wrong. Along came a pickup truck from the north. A driver, age 53, male, noticeably wasn't slowing down on his way to the light. We now know, he was on his phone.

My dad saw that the truck was racing head on to hit the woman and her child and hit the gas, putting his car in between the truck and the girls. The truck hit him on his driver side and that was that. Everyone but my dad lived. The man got arrested for reckless driving and is now facing manslaughter. The woman and her girl got to go home like nothing happened.

But my dad?... My mom didn't even make it in time to say goodbye. Now, here we are, driving to his funeral just 2 days later, a now broken family. On the day I was supposed to win my first state gold. I forfeited, of course. I could not care less, though. If nothing else, this made me see how unimportant track actually is in the scheme of life.

For some reason, I can't get my dad's words from that night out of head. I wonder if he overcame fear when he pressed that gas pedal to save those people, or if it was just an instant reaction?

For 2 days now, my stomach hasn't stopped hurting. My body feels like it's trying to make tears from somewhere now that I have cried so much that my eyes stopped making them.

I know my mom is in the same boat. She lost her high school sweetheart. Her husband. The father of her child. I think she's trying to be strong for me, but it hasn't worked very well. She wears her heart on her sleeve and yesterday I could hear her crying all day while I was locked in my own room doing the same.

One time I heard her walk up to my door to check on me. I hear a little "eepp" like she was trying to say some sort of word but couldn't over her tears... so she just walked away.

As we pull up to the funeral the pains in my belly get worse. I get nervous that someone is going to try and comfort me, tell me something like 'It's all going to be alright.' when I know that's not true. If there is anyway that today could not be the worst day of all time, it will be if nobody even talks to me.

We get out and take our seats. I put my head in my hands until things get started so I don't make eye contact with anyone. Certain people come up to my mom throughout to say things like 'I am so sorry.' and 'Let me know if you need anything.'

After a while, the service starts, and I keep my head in my hands the whole time. Like a bad dream, I am just waiting for it to be over. A sad song fills the room and photos start in a slide show. I wonder who its all for. Who's idea was it that this is the best way to comfort a grieving family. In actuality it just digs the knife deeper into my sole. So I just refuse to look up. When it finally ends, I feel a hand on my shoulder. Against my instincts, I look to see who it is. My mom, who got up from her seat next to me, is now standing in front of me.

Tears start to fill my eyes as I look at her. Who, now for the first time since the accident, finally isn't crying. I can see her blue eyes now clear from water. Her messy black hair and wrinkled clothes that she hasn't washed or changed in days. I wondered if people thought it rude for her to come her looking a mess, or if they would all get that how she looks is only a fraction of how bad she feels on the inside. I see her standing in front of me now ready to be THERE for me. Maybe the sad slide show was therapeutic for her where it wasn't for me. Made her think about the good times instead of dwelling of the bad? I can't be sure. Her life has been thrown off course. Is this her seeing it's possible to find another road?

She pulls me into her and hugs me and says "Rick, this is going to be the hardest thing we ever do... but it will be alright." And even though I did not want to hear that at all, I think the smallest part of me, deep down inside me... actually believed her.

Under her arm, we start to walk back to our car. When, on our way, out we get stopped by a woman that I don't recognize. With short blond hair parted in the middle. She has on a black skirt and black open toe shoes. Fitting for the nice spring day that it is. "Violet, right?" she says. She pans over to me and says "And you must be Rick." "Yes... did you know my husband?" My mom replies, hinting to me that she does not know the girl either.

"I... I am the woman that Paul saved that day... I understand if you don't want to see me, but... my family is alive because of your husband, and I would like to do whatever I can to help your family now... Even though I could never repay what he did."

Having listened to that, my mom seems taken back. After about 50 seconds of silence, she responds. "Thank you... I will think about it." Then, she pulls me, and we walk to the car. I ponder on if I appreciate what that woman was trying to do. On one hand, I am sure it took a little courage to come here today. On the other, I almost feel it would have been more compassionate to stay away as to not force us to be reminded of my dad's crash.

Still, my dad felt strongly enough to give his life to save her, the least I could do is give her a chance to get to know us. Then again, my dad didn't know anything about who this woman is. She could be a nut for all we know... but that didn't matter to him... In his eyes she was just someone that needed help. He would have done it for anyone.

The radio plays upbeat county music in the background on our otherwise quite drive home. I never much liked county music although it seems to be playing in every vehicle I have ever ridden in. In today's case, I welcome it. Focusing on the honkie tonk words of the song take my mind off the real world for a second and instead makes me wonder how someone got paid to write this stuff. Besides that, it helps drown out the silence.

We arrive at our house and walk inside. It's not a very big house by any means. A very cookie cutter, 3-bedroom, 2-bathroom, with the 3 rooms being quite small. Although, with just 2 of us living here now it seems larger than ever.

The 3rd room was dad's trophy room. It held all sorts of medals and awards won by both him and I. I haven't been in there since I put my new district medal in there. This small house now feels more like a giant labyrinth that mom and I are trying not to get lost in. One wrong step and you might see something that reminds you that this house can NEVER be a FULL home ever again.

Mom throws her keys on the counter. I guess I can get use to that. Dad used to follow her around to pick up after her as the day went on. He was always the neater of the two. "Hunny, I am going to throw a pizza in the oven. Do you wanna sit on the couch and eat it together?" she asks me.

I suppose I will have to get used to that, too. Mom did cook, but over the last couple years, grilling had become one of dad's major hobbies. It was not uncommon for us to eat steak or grilled chicken or a perfectly cooked burger 3 times a week.

"It's been a... long day. If it's alright with you, I think I'm just going to go to my room now." I tell her.

"Okay hunny, let me know if you need anything." She says back, but I can tell she wishes I would stay with her. Maybe I am being selfish. Maybe she needs me to be strong for her right now? I just don't know. The idea of being strong or doing anything at all just seems so out of reach right now.

I retreat to my room and sit on the bed. For a while I just sit and stare at the wall. Then I change my gaze to the shoe box I put in the corner. All white cleats with a gold stripe. They would have looked good at state. They were the 'surprise' that my dad texted me about his last day.

He was on his way back from getting them when the accident happened. Those stupid cleats. If it wasn't for them, maybe he would still be here! If it wasn't for me having made a dumb comment in front of him that I wanted a pair! What was wrong with the pair I had? Nothing, that's what! 'STUPID AND CARLESS' I think to myself as I pick up the box and throw it with all my might against the wall.

It hits with a crash before it falls to the floor, the soft cardboard having done no damage at all to my drywall. I may as well have just punched my pillow. I sit back down on top of the light blue comforter that covers my bed. With nothing else to do. No other emotions I feel like trying to comprehend that I'm feeling today. I just lay back, let my head hit the pillow, and close my eyes.

I sleep for what feels like all of spring and wake up at some point in July. Every day, rinse and repeat the same thing, subtract the rinse as somedays I can't be bothered to shower. I spend most of my days watching sit-coms in my room, only making a run to the kitchen for a sandwich and bowl of ice cream a few times a day. Although the ice cream mom buys doesn't come close to Scotty's, the thought of getting out of the house and actually going there seems daunting.

My mom seems to be improving. She's talking about going back to work soon. She doesn't have to as my father did have life insurance, so we are ok to lay around and morn for a while longer. However, she keeps saying how getting back to life as normal would be good for us.

How could it be normal with such a big piece of it now gone? She keeps telling me how my track coach has been calling and asking if I am going to be attending summer training. To be honest, it crossed my mind. I do miss running and jumping, but every time I think of track… I think of my dad… it's just too painful. I tell my mom to let the coach know that not only will I not attend summer training, but I won't be there during the school year either… I'm off the team.

CHAPTER 3

Driveway Therapy Sessions

"Is he home?" I hear a voice I recognize all too well at the front door speaking with my mother.

"He is in his room. Come on in, I am sure he'll be happy to see you, Wyatt." she responds, and I start to hear footsteps coming my way. Coming closer and closer to my room like thunder signaling that a storm is approaching.

My door slowly creeks open. "Rick, Wyatt is here to talk to you." mom says to me. I look over from under the covers of my bed while my video game 'The Four Kingdoms of Native's Point' keeps playing on my tv.

"Hey man… How you been?" he asks me while I watch mom slip out of the door and leave us alone. "I'm alright, man. What about you?" I say, trying to take the conversation away from me. He looks a little surprised by my response and says "Good, good…Ava and I have just been missing hanging out with you. You haven't answered any of my texts so I thought I would just come over here and invite you out tonight instead." he says with a hopeful smile. Going out does not sound like a good time, so instead I just put my eyes back on my tv and say "I would, man, but Autem is about to invade my kingdom… I better just stay here and beat this game."

"Yeah... yeah, I heard its good... Haven't got a chance to play it yet... I actually just got a job at Scotty's." he says to me. I look back over to him finally to crack a light smile. The thought of my friend Wyatt, the slacker, working in a little ice cream boy uniform, does make me want to go see that in person.

"Yeah, my dad got me a car. He said all I have to do is make a few payments to him this summer and then I can keep it. So, it's been scooping ice cream for me since May." May? Has it really been that long since I have seen him? Some friend I must be. "No way man? That's awesome! Did you drive it here?" I ask.

"Yes, I did in fact" he says with a full of confidence attitude. "Wanna go see it?" I think about it for a second before saying anything. No, I don't want to leave the house, but... it's just the driveway. How bad could it be? "Do I wanna see it? Of course, I wanna see it brother!" I say to him with a smile, and we leave my room to make our way to the driveway.

That's when I lay eyes on it. Its blue paint is flaking away revealing the grey steel underneath. Its rusty rims held up by its bald tires. And a nice dent right on the backdoor driver side. This may be the saddest minivan that I have ever seen. Almost makes me wonder if Wyatts dad is punishing him for something.

"She's not the prettiest, I know, but she gives me something beautiful." Wyatt says with a smirk.

"Oh yeah, what's that?" I indulge him.

"Sweet, sweet freedom, of course."

"Oh yeah? What's your curfew, Mr. Freedom?"

He looks like the question was a jab to the mid-section. "9 pm on school nights, 10 on weekends." he revels to me. I laugh a bit, but not too much. I have definitely missed hanging out with him. I realize that now.

"It's great, Wyatt. I'm sure Ava loves it." I tell him. He laughs and says, "Oh yeah, she loves the change of pace." See, Ava is from a more well-off family than the likes of us. She's used to riding around with her parents in much fancier rides. Though, with as down to earth as she is, you wouldn't know it by talking to her.

"Speaking of Ava, I better be going. I have to get ready if we're going to hangout tonight... You sure you don't want to come?" asks Wyatt. I think about it. Talking to him today has helped take my mind off things, but I am not sure I am ready for all the excitement of going out. I frantically look around seeing if I can offer him a counteroffer. My eyes land on the basketball hoop hanging over my garage.

"Any chance that you would want to stay and shoot around a bit instead? Ava is welcome to come by too." I say to him. He looks relieved that I asked him to stay and responds "Of course, man. Only if you're wanting to lose, that is? I'll text Ava and reschedule, we can just have a boy's night. She won't mind."

I know that is going to inconvenience him, but I let him reschedule. I didn't realize how much I needed a friend today. I go into the garage and start digging around until I find an old worn-out basketball. I bring it out and chuck up a shot. It gets close but bounces off the rim. Wyatt then grabs the rebound and walks back to 3-point range. "Check this out." he smirks. He then jumps and shoots the ball. It fly's though the air, banks of the backboard, and goes thought the hoop.

"Nice shot, man!" I exclaim, "How about a game of horse, if you think you can keep it up?"

"Like I said before, as long as you want to lose."

We play a game. After that, we play a few more, until the sun starts to drop lower. After a while, we're all tied up at H-O-R-S. I know this is likely the last game of the night, so I don't want to lose. Wyatt has been killing me with the 3-pointers up to this point. Who knew he could hoop this well. I know he spends a lot of time playing quick shot basketball at the arcade, but I never would have thought it would translate to real life like this.

It's my turn to shoot. I need to do something that is sure to win me the game. I start doing quick math in my head as an idea hits. The rim is at 10 feet. I am 5'8. When I reach out, that gives me another couple feet. So, let's say close to 7'8. That means I only have to jump 28 inches to the rim. I can definitely do that. The question is, can I jump high enough over that 28 inches to get the ball up and over? Worth a shot, here we go for the win!

I start making strides toward the basket. It reminds me of the run to the bar in the high jump. For a brief moment, the driveway of my cookie cutter subdivision home feels like a stadium full of people. I get close and jump off my right leg, holding the ball with both hands as I don't think I could grip it with just one. Soaring through the air, the rim and the top of my head almost meet the same height level. I am surprised at just how high up I got. I then proceeded to slam the ball down in the hoop and land on my feet.

Wyatt sands there with his jaw dropped. "I didn't know you could do that." He says. "I didn't know either." I say back, hyped up from my first dunk.

"Well, I guess you win because I am not following up that." He laughs. He looks at his phone "It's 8:43 anyway, I better start on my way home... but, you want to play again tomorrow?"

"Yeah. Sure thing, man. Thanks for stopping by... it helped to see a friend." I say. He gives me a salute before he gets in his van and drives off.

That feeling of running and jumping... it made me feel like me again, just for the afternoon. Not to mention how normal it felt to be joking around with Wyatt again. Maybe I am not as done with sports as I thought.

CHAPTER 4

Back To School

Wyatt kept coming over since that day in July. Almost every day, actually. Just as surely as the page on the calendar flipped from July to August, our basketball skills got just a little better every day. Before I knew it, I was out training my dunks and ball handling until dark every night.

Our games of horse moved to one-on-one games where we each had to use all of our skills and effort to get one over on each other. Hey, it may just be one month of playing right now, but the idea of thinking we have a real shot of making our high school's basketball team is starting to build a home somewhere in the back of my brain. I wonder how I could compare to the existing players. I know I bring a level of athleticism, but would that be enough to close the gap of kids that have been playing for years? I am not sure if I'll try out yet. If I do I will need to lean on a lesson my dad taught me... hard work and determination can overcome more than you think possible. He would always say something like that when I would doubt myself in track season.

High school. Today marks the gut punching reality that I can't just hide away in my room/driveway for the rest of my life. I'm waiting in my driveway for Wyatt to pick me up for our first day of junior year. I tried my very best to convince my mom I had a stomachache, but she wouldn't go for it. So, here I am.

I didn't feel the need to get dressed up and look nice for the first day, like I normally do. Just athletic shorts and a pullover hoodie. Gracing my feet are my cheap dollar store slides, with a pair of black socks on. I figured today will take all my energy, so I didn't want to waste any on finding the perfect outfit. I wouldn't have even fixed my hair if it wasn't for my mom chasing me down with gel, yelling "YOU ARE NOT LEVING THE HOUSE LOOKING LIKE THAT." She then promptly slicked my jet-black hair back, making me look like I was plucked right out of the roaring 20's.

Soon enough, I see Wyatts van pull up, and I hop in. I take a look at him to note that he has not put any extra effort into his outfit either. Baggy jeans and a T-shirt, as per usual. He greats me with a smirk saying, "Hey, bro. Nice hair." I take my hand and re-mess up my hair, shaking it out until I look back to being like I am from the modern era. "Thanks for the ride." I tell him. He nods and we start on our way to school.

"So, you ready for the first day?" he asks me. I give him my honest thoughts on the matter "As ready as I'll ever be I suppose. It's going to be a long day full of 'Hey rick, you doing okay?' then I'll have to throw on a smile and act as if everything is just jolly…"

"Yeah, I get you… So… Are you doing okay?"

I give him an eye roll and say "Oh yeah, just jolly."

"Come on, man it's me. You can be honest with me." he tells me. I think about it and as much as sharing my feelings seems kind of lame, he is right. I don't know how much my mom can handle talking about this stuff so if I can't talk to him… who can I talk to?

"I don't really know if I am doing okay… I mean it's been months since it happened now. I guess I am adjusting, finding a little joy in a few things. I just miss him... I think any kid without a parent would tell you it feels like something is just missing."

"I know it's gotta be hard. Just keep trying to find those little moments of joy, and remember, me, Ava, especially your mom I'm sure... where all here for you."

I give him a nod. "Thanks... I do appreciate it." Speaking of Ava, we pull up to the school and she is waiting outside to walk in with us. As we walk up to her, I notice she did in fact take the time to look nice for the first day. She has on a sundress, white flat bottom shoes and her hair pulled to the side showing off some new earrings.

She waves as we get close. She gives Wyatt a hug and then greets me as it has been a second since we've seen each other. "Hey Rick... you doing okay?" she asks. I look at Wyatt and say "What did I tell ya? Word for word." He immediately starts laughing and a confused Ava asks "What? Did I say something wrong?"

"You're fine." I tell her. "And to answer your question, I am jolly," I say, which keeps Wyatt's laughter going on longer. The bell rings and we head off to the first class of the day.

I'm not lucky enough to have a friend in my first hour class so I sit in the back by myself hoping no one tries to take the seat next to me.

"C'mon Shelby, wear my jersey this Friday." I hear from the front of the class. I look to see a large man in the front of the class. He must be a senior. Gotta be a decent amount over six foot and by the size of his shoulders I am surprised he fit though the door.

"You know, John, if you spent as much time practicing your free throws as you do trying to get me to wear your jersey, you might have made more than 20% of them last year." Now that voice I recognize...as anyone in our school would. Shelby Cuningham. She's who most people in our school would consider to be the best athlete in school. She's the star point guard of our girls' basketball team and is ranked top 25 in the nation.

People are already trying to project what WNBA team she will end up on. "Ah, I don't care about free throws right now. Its football season and that sack record is as good as mine." John responds.

Just then, the teacher walks in and everyone scrambles to their seats. As he writes algebra 2 on the white board, I think '20% from the free throw line? I feel like I have to be able to do better than that. I have never actually gone to go watch our basketball team play but it sounds like they may be in desperate need of some help.'

The rest of the day goes pretty smoothy. No big problems to speak of, just the odd sad look in my direction every once in a while. I made it to the end though and that's what matters. I've just got to keep the strength up to go back tomorrow.

Wyatt drops me back off at home and I grab my ball from my garage. I take 13 steps from under the rim and drop a stick to mark a free throw line. I start hitting shots and I'm not doing too bad when my mom comes out of the house.

"Rick, I didn't hear you pull in... How was school?" she asks. I tell her "Ah, you know, I never have loved going to school... but it wasn't as bad as I had built up in my head."

"Good, good" she says. "Well, I'll get dinner started soon."

"Ok... I think I am going to stay out here until I can hit 7 out of 10 of these shots in a row." I tell her. She waits at the door for a second and says "How about I stay out here and watch... Then when you get 7 out of 10, we can go get dinner out? Maybe visit your friend at Scotty's for dessert?" I've got to admit, that does sound good. I think about what Wyatt told me about looking for the little moments of joy and say "Yeah, mom, that sounds great."

Just a few months ago I thought my days of getting victory ice cream were forever over... but today, I think whether it's taking first at a track meet or hitting shots in the driveway. Or maybe it's just realizing you're not alone and you have people that care about you. Maybe you can find a little victory in every day.

CHAPTER 5

Seasons Change

The nice October breeze brings leaves into my driveway that skate by my ever-shifting feet. Wearing a hoodie for our newly acquired cold weather, I have my arms spread out wide in attempts to guard Wyatt from making it to the hoop.

The score is 20- 18 with me wining our game to 21. I play close defense as he dribbles the ball in his back hand, keeping it away from me. As long as I stop the 3, I'll get a chance to score. However, that's easier said than done.

He takes a quick step back to put him beyond our mark for the three-point line and I know he going for the step back 3. I jump with my hands up in an attempt to block it, only to be surprised when instead of shooting it he dribbles right past me to the basket and lays the ball right in for 2 points.

I hear clapping from the sideline. "Way to go sweetie!" Ava calls from my front porch. Wyatt smiles back at her. "Sweetie? What are you 90?" I ask.

Wyatt tosses the ball to me "Check up." he says. I take the ball and toss it back to him for the check. "Try to keep up, Sweetie." I jokingly say to him with a wink.

I begin to dribble back and forth between my legs seeing if I can get him to bite on anything so I can get by him, but he sticks to me like glue.

Wyatt did something I wasn't used to, to score last time. His game is evolving, he's getting more well-rounded. I think maybe I should try to do the same and shoot a 3. My ball handling has improved a lot since I have been playing, and my shot has some as well, though I can't seem to figure out the exact science as to why. Realizing what actions I do that make my shot better or worse has been difficult for me.

Oh well, you miss every shot you don't take. Right? I dribble hard with my right hand and flinch with my body to fake like I am going to drive in. He bites ever so slightly, so when I pick the ball up and jump back behind the 3-point mark I have enough room to shoot my shot.

I jump high to make sure I clear his attempt to block and let the ball leave my hand at my highest point. As the ball flies though the air my hopes are high that I can sink it and win the game. However, as it gets closer and closer, I can tell the path it's taking is off.

Sure enough, it hits the backboard and falls to the right side of the rim, not even touching the rim itself. Which means it's all too easy for Wyatt to grab the ball and throw it back in for a lay up to win the game.

Clapping again from Ava on the sideline. "I knew you could do it honeybunny!" Okay, now I think she's being wince on purpose. Wyatt gives me a cocky smile "What? You don't have any jokes now?"

"None at all, you earned that win, Sweetie." I say back to him. He laughs. "Joke all you want, but a deal's a deal. I won, so that means you have to come with me and Ava to the last football game tonight."

Ugh. I've been winning much more than losing lately so I thought that making that deal would be nothing more than a formality. Although it's true, going to school every day is starting to get easier day by day, but I think I have just grown accustom to being at home in my free time.

I am sure Wyatt has noticed that I am still part hermit crab clinging desperately to my shell. That's most likely why he has kept making attempts to get me out of the house. As much as I don't really want to attend, he is right… a deal is in fact a deal, so my hands are tied.

"Alright, alright." I tell him. "Let me just grab a jacket from inside. It's supposed to get cold tonight." He nods and I head into the house to retrieve my coat. I grab one from my room and go to head out through the door by the kitchen. On my way, I find my mom sitting at the table reading a book.

She's in the sweats she normally sleeps in, and I can't help but notice the self-help title of the book. 'HOW TO GET BACK UP AGAIN'

"Good read?" I ask her. She looks up at me like I spooked her and tells me "Eh, I am not really getting much out of it… I just figured there has to be some reason people buy this stuff."

I nod a little bit not really knowing what to say next. "Anyway, what do you want for dinner? I can get something cooking and we can watch some TV?" she asks me with a faint amount of excitement in her voice.

Things have been going well between us lately. I have been out of my room more and we have been spending more time together at home, as neither of us are too fond of leaving.

"Actually, I think I am going to go to the football game tonight…" I say. For a half a second, her face turns sour before it changes to a smile letting me know that she is actually a little sad she's going to spend the night alone. Although what she says is "Really? That's great! You'll have fun!… Just call me if you think you'll be out real late please."

"Yeah, I will." I say as I start to leave. Before I grab the door handle, I feel her grab my shoulder. She pulls me in for a goodbye hug. I hug her back then I head out.

I walk out to the back door of Wyatt's van and jump in as him and Ava are already inside waiting on me. "Alright, I'm ready." I say, and we take off to head to the game.

Upon arriving and walking into the stadium, we clearly feel the temperature drop. It's an especially cold, late October night. I can hear the game roaring loudly before we are even in clear view of the field. We walk past an outrageous long line for the concessions stand advertising hot chocolate for sale.

"Hey Rick, me and Ava will grab us some hot chocolate to keep us warm if you head up and find us a place to sit?" Wyatt asks me. "You're going to wait in that? The game will be over before you finally get our drinks." I say back to him.

"Well, I'm not going to sit out in the cold all night without them." Ava responds.

"Fine. I'll meet you guys up there." I say as I turn to go into the unkept jungle that is a high school bleachers student section. After searching and weaving pass countless of my peers, I find a free spot to sit big enough for 3 or 4 people. I take my seat in the middle of it and do my best to man spread and look unapproachable to avoid anyone trying to steal the seats I am trying to save for my friends.

I do my best to pay attention to the game. Right now, we're losing in a close one. It's 7-10 as half time is coming up. No surprise it's low scoring, I have heard all year about how good our defense is. "Another sack for number 91 John Lynn. The senior is closing in on all-time sack record for West Des Moine high school! If he gets two more this game, it's all his!" the announcer yells out.

John Lynn is the giant I have my first hour class with. No wonder the opponent's offensive line can't hold him back. I shiver in my seat trying to fight the cold, when my friends finally decide to join me with hot drinks in hand. "Here, I brought a large blanket we can wrap around us." Ava states. As so, they sit. Wyatt to my left and Ava to his left. We're huddled up with a blanket on our backs and hot chocolate in our hands, just watching a close game and enjoying each other's company.

I start to feel happy I came, like I am in the middle of a time in my life where I should really be able to appreciate just having friends and low responsibilities. The half time whistle blows, and the teams head off to the locker rooms leaving us to an intermission.

"Ava!" I hear a girl's voice call out and turn to Ava waving at someone heading towards us. I look over to see just who it could be and am surprised to see that its none other than Shelby Cunningham approaching, wearing a jersey that has a big 9-1 on it, John Lynn's number.

Her curly hair is pulled into a bun, and our schools colors are painted on her face over her brown skin. "It's good to see you!" she says walking up to Ava's side.

Wyatt's confused look makes me think he doesn't know who Shelby is. "Good to see you as well!" Ava responds. She then takes the time to introduce everyone. "Guys, this is Shelby, we're lab partners." Ah, so that explains this unlikely friendship. She keeps talking "Shelby, this is my boyfriend Wyatt and our friend Rick."

Shelby then looks over at me and says, "Ah, yes, the famous track star himself."

I awkwardly chuckle, not so much knowing how to respond to that. "Er... uh ... not so much anymore actually."

"Oh really, why not?" she says. Does she really not know what happened? Or is she just playing naïve? I can't tell. I brush it off and say "Well, it just so happens me and Wyatt are putting our time into getting ready for basketball tryouts this year instead."

Her smile brightens "Really??" she looks back to Ava "I guess that means you'll be coming to the games?! That's great news! I need someone to sit with. We play right before the boys and none of my teammates ever stay and watch." Ava nods.

Then our conversation is interrupted by the start of the second half getting under way. "Another sack by Lynn! He has now tied the record!" the intercom blurts out.

I look at Shelby while she's cheering "You changed your mind about wearing his jersey, I see." I say to her. "Oh, yeah." she giggles "The goofball talked me into it, said he was sure to break the sack record if I wore it."

"Looks like it's working." I respond. A little while later in the fourth quarter of the game, the offence takes the field. Our QB throws a deep pass that gets grabbed by one of our best players. "Matt Carder makes the catch on the sideline for a 54 yard gain! The Stags are in the red zone!" we hear over speakers.

Then, right after, I hear something that changes my whole night. It's Matt's father cheering for him in the stands in front of us. "Your son sure is having a heck of a game, Dan!" another fan says to Matt's dad. "He wants this win bad. I promised him a new pair of cleats if they make it past districts this year!" he says back, and the two laugh.

Are new cleats some rite of passage when you have success in your sport or is this just a coincidence. Some sick joke that's getting played on me.

Like a plane getting shot down, my mind goes from smooth sailing to crashing and burning in an instant. Will this happen every time things start to go good for me? Every time I claw my way up the mountain of happiness, will I just be kicked back down it by the fact that I will never again know a father's love? And the slap in the face is that the reason why is that I wasn't content with something as minor as the cleats I already had?

I sit in silence the rest of the game just waiting to be brought home, swimming in the fiery blaze that is guilt and anxiety the whole time. After what feels like way too long, the game does end. A 10-13 loss for the Stags.

We start the car ride home and I remain in peril on the way. After dropping Ava off, we reach my house and pull into the driveway. It's late but my guess is that my mom stayed up to make sure that I made it home safely. "What a great night!" Wyatt says, "Sucks we lost but hey, still a fun time at the game."

I've been dead silent up to this point in the ride back so I think he can tell something is up. I don't mean to be such a buzz kill but it feels like a little flame in my brain has turned into a blazing fire with the realization that I had earlier at the game. And that fire... I can't seem to put it out... I just want to put it out.

"Wyatt, can I ask you something." I say to him.

"Yeah... anything man." he replies.

"If anything were to ever happen to me, I want you to go visit my mom every once in a while... If I'm gone, she'll have no one else"

"Rick, nothing's going to happen to you."

"I'm sure that's what my dad thought."

"It was a freak accident, Rick. The chances are so low of another freak accident happening to you."

My face turns as stern as I can make it, so he knows I'm serious and I tell him "I just need you to promise me."

He looks at me like he's trying to read me. To make sense of what I'm telling him.

"No," he says.

"Why the heck not!" I say with base in my voice.

"I won't do it!" his voice gets louder.

"WHY!"

"Because you're not going anywhere! I don't know if this is your way of telling me you're thinking of doing something stupid, but you're not going to do that! Your mom needs YOU Rick! Not me! Never mind the fact that your friends need you too! If you ask me, the whole world needs Rick Joseph in it, so you're not going anywhere! Like it or not!"

I put my head down and stare at my knees. "So YOU need to promise ME," he continues "nothing is going to happen to you... I'll stay in this car with you as long as it takes until you promise"

The first tear falls from my hanging face, and then the water starts pouring out. With every drop that comes it feels to be finally extinguishing the fire in my head. And clarity peaks through in the form of tough love that I needed to hear. Tough love that no one other than Wyatt has yet to be brave enough to give me.

"I'm sorry... I promise... I'm so sorry" I say crying. I don't even know who I am apologizing to. Wyatt for putting something so heavy on him. Or my dad for moping around and not living the joyful life he would have given anything to protect.

As I sob, I feel Wyatt's arm wrap around me. And with the night above us he just sits there with me for what feels like hours until I'm all out of tears to cry.

CHAPTER 6

Try Outs

Only the weekend was given to mourn the season ending loss of our football team. Now, on this Monday, basketball season has been eagerly waiting to get underway.

Some of the basketball team's key players also played football so it didn't make sense to start up practice until they could join. Unfortunately for the basketball team, it is very evident that football is our school's premier sport. After all, it is hard to make yourself great at something when you only practice it a few months of the year.

I, in fact, do aspire to be great. I shot all day yesterday before making an attempt to go to sleep at a good time to make sure I am ready for this tryout. That attempt didn't end up going so well for me, as I tossed and turned most of the night in anticipation for today. I haven't met the coach before, so I can only hope that he will view me as useful talent. I would assume being a state runner up level athlete as well as being able to dunk will be more than enough to get his attention, but there is no way to know for sure. School sports unfortunately all too often break down into a popularity contest. Or more accurately a how much money do your parents have contest. If the coach is a stain up guy I don't see that being a problem. With the teams record the last couple of years I would guess he can't afford not to play the best players.

I have got to give these tryouts my all. I think to myself as I walk into the gym. As I enter though the double doors, I see the backs of a crowd of people all staring at the school's medical trainers tending to a student on the ground under the basket.

I try and weave through to see who it is, but I can't get a good look. One of the disadvantages to being short is that I can't see over anyone. "Dude, did you see that?" I hear Wyatt, who was already in the gym, coming towards me. "No, I just got here," I say "Who got hurt?"

"It's Shelby." he says back. News that I was not expecting, I had almost forgotten that girl's tryouts were going on at the same time. Wyatt keeps talking "She was just going for a lay-up, nothing special about it at all. When she came down her knee popped so loud the whole room could hear it."

My face cringes just thinking about that kind of injury. I can only hope it sounds worse than it is. A big season ending injury could hurt her college chances.

We watch as they wheel her past us and out the door. All the while she groans in pain. After she is gone and out of the room, a man who must be the coach starts talking.

"As unfortunate as it, is injuries are a reality of this sport." he tells us bluntly, commanding the room. He's tall, in athletic wear, and has a dark mustache on his otherwise clean-shaven face. He looks to be somewhere around his late 40's but still seeming to be in good shape. I wonder if he hoops with the team often.

He continues "We still have a lot to get through today, so we better get to it. We had a lot of key players graduate last year. In fact, we only have 2 returning starters. That being, John Lynn and Matt Carder, who just came off an impressive football season. So, now is your time to show me you can make an impact on this team."

The chest of all the men in the room start to puff out as chips appear on our shoulders. All of us eager to show we have what it takes to join the starting five.

We line up to start with dribbling drills, which I expect to excel at. The kid right in front of me in line, I don't recognize. He's tall, must be around 6'1. He looks very athletic and looks to be Hispanic. He turns around to greet me with a half-smile and says "So, you think you're going to make it?" It's hard to tell if he is really asking because he's curious or if he's trying to make me second guess myself.

"I hope so." I say, keeping it short. "What about you?" I ask in return. His face gets more serious. "I KNOW so." he says. Again, not sure if he's trying to out confidence me, or if he treats every small talk like it's the most important conversation of his life.

His turn to dribble down the court comes up and he starts by catching a pass from the last guy that went. He goes down spam dribbling through the legs, in and out, and behind the back. All with impressive speed and control. Whoever he is, he clearly can handle a basketball quite well.

He hits a layup that goes in the basket nicely. Then chucks the ball back down the court to me. The pass goes wide left. I try to grab it, but it rolls out of bounds. Sloppy passing isn't the end of the world, but it's not going to win him any points.

I get the ball and start dribbling down the court. I keep it simple, going through the legs just once. I keep my eyes up pretending to look for pass targets, showing my worth as a point guard. When I get close to the rim, I hit a nice two step reverse layup that goes through with just one bounce of the rim. I then hit a strong arm pass that bullets into the chest of the person who is next up.

I go stand by the kid that was in front of me earlier. "What's your name?" I ask.

"AJ Matinez. That was a nice pass just now." He tells me.

"Thanks, I'm Rick." deciding to give him my name even though he didn't ask for it. On the court we see the kid behind me dribble the ball into his shoe sending it rolling off. "Well, Rick." AJ says, "Looks like our odds are looking pretty good."

"Aright, everyone line up at half court!" couch yells. "For our next drill I want to see how you play when the odds are not on your side. Chances are, at some point this season you'll have to play against someone who is faster and stronger than you are. So today you all are going to get the chance to do just that. Each of you is going to do a one-on-one vs John Lynn. Now, John was first team all defense last year, so I am not expecting anyone to actually score on him. I want to test how well you react to adversity. That being said, you have one shot each so make it count."

John takes the court standing on the free throw line, his blond hair hanging on his forehead cut short above his eyes. He's sporting a t-shirt with the sleeves cut off showing off arms much larger than my own. This is not surprising considering how full of himself he seems. Nevertheless, trying to score on a kid that big is intimidating.

"Who wants to try first?" John says, holding his arms out doing his best impression of Russell Crowe in Gladiator. The volume in the room turns down. Everyone would rather try to take their shot when John has already gone a few rounds, get him when he's tried.

"I'll go." I hear Wyatt's voice from the crowd of basketball players in the room. As he steps forward, John announces "Oh great, the stoner." The coach raises his eyebrow. Wyatt awkwardly chuckles "Not a stoner coach... just dress like one."

Coach stays quiet, not laughing at the joke. Wyatt steps up to the 3-point line. The view of skinny 5'10 Wyatt standing in front of buff 6'4 John is a mismatch if I've ever seen one.

The whole room is expecting Wyatt to be made a fool of himself as they take stance. Wyatt bounce passes the ball to

John doing a check. John passes right back to him. As soon as the ball touches Wyatts hands that will mean the game is on.

It bounces up to the chest of Wyatt. He grabs it and in the blink of an eye jumps pulling up a 3-point shot. John tries to jump to block but he definitely wasn't expecting Wyatt to shoot right off rip like that. John's jump is too little too late as the ball flies past his fingertips, making a nice arch on its way to the basket.

It flies right through the rim not even hitting it. John turns around scanning the room in disbelief "Well, I guess there's no stopping that." He says, shrugging his shoulders. Nice that he's being a good sport about it.

"Well, that didn't take long. Good job Mr. Herbert" coach says. Wyatt gets patted on the back by everyone on his way back to take his seat. "Alright, so I am a little out of practice. Who's next?" John announces.

I take a deep breath. I can't let Wyatt show me up too bad. I guess now is as good as time as any. "I'll try my hand." I volunteer, stepping up to the 3-point line.

John grabs the ball checking to me, and the game is on. I don't trust my 3 ball like Wyatt does. I'm going to have to get in close. John is right on me from the start. He clearly doesn't want to be scored on again. "C'mon John, don't let 'em past you." I hear John's fellow senior Matt Carder yell from the sideline.

I dribble hard with my right hand and then try to get pass him by crossing to my left. He stays tight to me. For a big guy, he's much faster than I thought. I try everything to get by him and each time I run into either his shoulder or chest that feels like a brick wall.

I think I must be running out of time. If there was a shot clock going, it would be winding down. However, I seem to be stuck at the 3-point line. How embarrassing. I've got to think quick. He must be expecting me to throw up a shot from here just because I can't drive in. He's going to want to block it in case I happen to make a lucky shot.

I ride the 3-point line with an idea in my head. I take a step back fast to get just a little bit of space. He steps forward to meet me. I do a hesitation step where I hold the ball in my hand just for a second, not long enough to count as a carry so that I am still free to dribble. Me picking up the ball gives the illusion that I'm going to shoot.

John jumps to stop my fake giving me the time I need to blow right past him. He was so focused on not giving up a 3 pointer that he bit on my fake just like I thought he would. I run up and take a big leap as get to the basket. Bringing down a simple 2 hand dunk.

Cheers start up in the crowd of kids watching. "YOU'RE KIDDING!" an angry John yells. Sure, he was a good sport about getting a surprise 3 shot on him, but a short kid dunking on him in front of everyone… that's got to hurt the ego.

I go take my seat next to Wyatt and we watch as the rest of the kids take their turns. None of them having any luck, John goes the rest of the tryouts undefeated, making me and Wyatt feel all the more accomplished.

As tryouts wrap up, coach calls names off a list he has. My name and Wyatts, as well as AJ, that I met earlier being included in the list. Everyone not on the list leaves the gym.

"Alright gentlemen, for those of you who don't know me yet, my name is coach Morgan. I look forward to getting to know you all better this season. Welcome to the West Des Moine Stags high school basketball team!"

CHAPTER 7

Team Bonding

My track suit is doing its best to keep me warm on this chilly 48-degree morning. Though my fingertips hurt a little bit from the cold temperatures mixed with the basketball slamming against them as we play at the outdoor court of our local park.

A lot of my teammates where smart enough to bring sock hats. While me, on the other hand, has the tops of my ears red from cold wind I catch running down the court. The court that we had to broom all the leaves off before we could start our practice this morning as early November is finally upon us, As the branches on the trees become bare, so it signals that our first game is drawing near.

Today is a Saturday. We wouldn't normally be practicing today but coach Morgan insisted that park basketball followed by lunch together would bring much needed comradery between the team.

We are in the middle of a five-on-five pickup game. Our 15-man team was split up into 3 teams of 5. Games are to 21, winner stays in. The team Wyatt was placed on played the team John Lynn was placed on first where John's team won 21-9. John himself had 12 points in the paint. He really must have been trying to get revenge for his loss at the try outs.

Right now, my team is playing John's in a game that I am losing 14-16. I'll admit, the only reason the game is so close is due to me having AJ Martinez on my team. Throughout practicing with him this last week I have learned that not only is he just a freshman, but he is a real threat with the ball in his hands.

As I bring the ball down the court, I see him cut in on the left wing. I hit him with a sharp pass that splits the gap between 2 defenders. One of which, being senior Matt Carder. I hit AJ right in the chest as he nears the left side of the free throw line. He grabs the catch and hits a snap back jump shot that looks as smooth as butter getting space from his defender and hitting the mid-range shot nicely. Score is now tied up at 16 a piece.

"Good shot, AJ." Coach Morgan yells out "Try and focus on releasing the ball at the highest point in your jump. If that defender were any taller, he may have been able to block you."

Unfortunately for all of AJ's worth on offence, he doesn't shine as well on defense. He tries to cover Matt, but with as loose as the converge is, it prompts Matt to hit an all too wide open 3 pointer once he brings the ball down the court. Score is now 16-19.

Ball back in my hands, I know I got to make something out of this play. I start bringing the ball up and as I approach half court, I notice the defense has changed their strategy. Now for some reason, John has moved up to guard me.

This is odd, considering he's a center who would typically be playing under the basket. For him to be all the way up past half court, he must have some sort of plan. Maybe he plans on trying to steal the ball and get away with a fast break to win it? I dibble the ball with my left hand and put my right shoulder between John and I, forcing him to reach farther if he does try to nab the ball from me.

As I approach the half court line, I try to make a quick move to get by him. Hoping to find AJ open when I have enough space to pass. Just as I cross the half court, John lowers his shoulder and checks it into me like he's aiming to bust through a locked door, knocking me back to the other side of half court and on my butt in the process. "OOOO!" I hear the collective reaction from the sidelined players, followed their laughter.

"What the heck man? That's a blocking foul!" I snap back at John, who's towering over me while I'm on the ground. "Blocking foul?" he says, pretending to be confused. He looks back at the half court line and says "Looks like a back court violation to me… Our ball."

I look over to coach Morgan who has been observing the game. So sure that he would side with me, he says "Rick, you should have passed the ball earlier or waited until you had more space to cross. A ref won't always side with you when you're playing the line like that. I'm going to give the ball to John's team so you don't create bad habits doing that."

"Tienes que estar bromeando!" an angry AJ blurts out in his natural language. John smirks as he takes the ball back to his side of the court. I hang back clinching my fist. If I don't want to lose this game, I need to get a stop here.

John throws the ball in to an open Matt. AJ tries to full court guard him. He must just be trying to make up for the points he gave up last play. Things don't work out like he hoped, however. Matt hits him with a dirty cross that almost brakes AJ's ankles. AJ just barley manages to stay on his feet, but Matt blows right by him. Dribbling down with a wide-open court in front of him. All that stands in between Matt and winning this game… is me. He charges in and I meet him under the basket. He jumps up with the ball in hand, going for a lay up to win it.

I give my jump all the power my legs can muster. If I can reach above the rim, I might be able to block it. My jump is good. I am as high as I need to be for the block. I reach my hand up expecting to swat down the loose ball, but to my surprise Matt didn't let go of it. This isn't a layup at all… He's going for a dunk?!

My hand does nothing to slow down the ball as he shoves it through the rim. Knocking me to the ground for the second time this game. A dunk? No way. I thought I was the only one on this team that could pull that off.

Matt, at least, reaches his hand out to help me, unlike John. Which I try to appreciate, despite being pissed off about my defeat.

"Alright, John's team wins." coach Morgan says. "Time for lunch. Everybody to the picnic area."

We all head over to the picnic tables that seat 6 each. Just as we are about to take our seats next to our own little clicks amongst the team coach announces. "Woah, not so fast. I will be assigning seats."

Some of us look puzzled while others hang their heads in disappointment, figuring that this is likely some sort of plan to encourage us to bond with our less likable team members.

"At table one" coach continues "John Lynn, Matt Carder, AJ Martinez, Wyatt Herbert, and Rick Joseph." Here we go, I think to myself. At least I have Wyatt with me. We sit down with our lunch boxes as coach seats the rest of the team at different tables.

Wyatt, AJ, and I all sit on one side of the table with John and Matt facing us. The 6th seat remains open. The lunch starts pretty quiet until Matt breaks the silence "Yo freshman," he says referring to AJ "heard you blurting out some sort of Spanish or something out there. Where you from?"

AJ chokes down a bite of his sandwich before answering. "Venezuela actually. Lived there until my family moved to the states when I was 9. Since then, we've kind of bounced around. Parents looking for steady work, you know how it is."

"Right on, right on. Had some nice moves out there. I'm sure you'll get some playing time this year."

"Yeah... would have won too... if it weren't for that blocking foul coach let slide. You ask me he needs his eyes checked."

After that comment by AJ, John looks at me and smiles while chewing his food and says "Don't blame me. Maybe if you try and pack on a little more muscle, you might be able to get across center court bub."

"Woah, easy there, farm boy. No need for insults. It was a good game, you both should be happy." Wyatt interjects. Probably trying to make sure I don't say something that would get my butt kicked.

"Alright everyone, I put you at the tables I did for a reason." Coach starts to speak, putting our conversation on hold. "Table one, congratulations... you are the starters for our first game. Table two, you will be the backups. Table three you will be on reserve."

AJ, Wyatt, and I all hit fist bumps happy about the good news. John and Matt don't change their expressions as I'm sure they were expecting this being starters last year and all.

"Now, I am going to come around to each table with this sheet of paper. You're going to pass it around and write what number you want to be so I can get jerseys ordered." Coach Morgan says.

Coach makes his way over to our table and takes a seat. "John, Matt, same numbers as last year? 91 and 2?" he asks. John hits him with a nod "Yes coach."

"AJ?" coach asks.

"21 sir, same as last 1st round draft pick from Venezuela. Greivis Vasquez. I intend to do the same thing!" AJ says with a certain confidence about him.

"Uh huh." Coach responds sounding uninterested in AJ's little spiel. "Herbert?"

"Can I go with 0 coach?" Wyatt asks.

"Someone has a need to be different, I see... Alright, 0 it is. That just leaves Rick... What number you want, bud?"

I think about it for a brief moment before answering "I'll do 36 coach."

"You got it, thank you boys." coach says, getting up and heading to the next table. Wyatt taps me on the shoulder and asks, "You looked unsure, did you just pick 36 at random?"

I let out a soft laugh and shrug. "Yeah... just didn't know what to pick." I tell him. It's not true though. I have been thinking about what my number would be for a while now, and there is really only one number that means anything to me. 36, it's how old my dad was.

I won't tell anyone why I picked that number, but if he is looking down on me from somewhere... I want him to know, even if it's not track anymore, in my head, he'll be with me on the court as well.

CHAPTER 8

Group Hang

The following Monday we hit the ground running practicing together as a starting 5. One week of running plays together helped us come close to hitting some sort of rhythm. Unfortunately, not a rhythm I would much like to listen to.

AJ would spend a lot of time and energy doing flashy dribbling to free up just a little bit of space and John would drive in and force a layup in the paint even if there's teammates open on the outside. As for me, playing point... I was having a hard time communicating things I saw on the court to my team. After all, I am from a more... individual sport.

Wyatt and I normally stayed late after practice for some extra shooting as our first game is on Monday and we wanted to make sure we were ready. I can tell I have been improving. Still the rate at which I do so is starting to slow down. When I first started playing I got noticeable better ever day it felt like. Now I am force to latch on to frustratingly small improvements. All that leads us to this Friday night.

Tonight, instead of staying after practice, Wyatt talks me into joining him and Ava at the local arcade. He said it would be good to blow off some steam before the big game. Gave me some spiel about how the more relaxed I am the better I'll play. Relaxing is the least of my concerns however. As we walk into the neon light filled game room to meet up with Ava, all I can really think about is how this first game is going to go.

My mindset changes however, when upon setting eyes on Ava, I notice she's not alone. Standing, or rather leaning over her crutches next to her, is Shelby with a cast over her injured knee.

It's going to be hard to relax if she's here. See, I am not the most social of butterflies. Wyatt and Ava are like my siblings at this point, I know I can be myself around them. However, with new people around, I tend to stumble over my words in a failing attempt to appear normal.

Still, I'll admit, looking at her smile and wave over to us as we walk closer to them… I'd be dumb to actually want her to leave.

"Hey guys." Wyatt says as we approach. "Shelby, I didn't know you were coming."

"Of course, had to come and celebrate Ava. Right?!" Shelby says back. Wyatt looks to Ava with a puzzled look. "Celebrate?" he asked.

"I have the highest GPA in the school over the first quarter." Ava says back to him, looking down at her feet as if it's not a big deal. If you know Ava, you know she is very driven in school and this news undoubtedly made her day. As good friends, a little pizza and arcade games is worth it to congratulate her. Unfortunately, it seems me and Wyatt were out of the loop on this one.

"No way! That's awesome Ava! Why didn't you tell me?" says Wyatt.

"I did, last night… You didn't respond." Ava says with an annoyed expression.

"Oh, I must not have seen it…"

"So, you just went over a full day without checking your texts from your girlfriend? Nice to know where I stand."

"Sorry, sorry. It's just ever since Rick and I became starters, I have been getting home late and tired and have just been crashing."

"You're starting!?" Ava perks up for just a second before remembering that she's mad at him. "When were you going to tell me you're starting? Seems like you two start playing basketball and just forget all about me!" she turns to include me in her scowl.

"No, it's not like that... Look, it seems we all have something to celebrate tonight. Why don't I order a pizza and some game cards, and we'll focus on having a good time tonight?"

Ava looks around at the visible discomfort that Shelby and I are feeling by being here for this conversation and says "Okay... we'll talk more about this later." Sparing us from the awkwardness.

Wyatt orders a large pepperoni, and we sit to eat. I am forced to sit on the same side of the booth as Shelby as the 'love birds' take the other side. I scoot in as far as I can and keep my elbows in as I eat as to not bump her. Wait, I don't want her to think I am avoiding her. Am I acting like the fact I am sitting next to her is appalling to me? See, this is what I mean when I say I over think around new people.

After we make happy plates and the pizza is all gone Wyatt says "Alright, we're going to play some ski-ball." referring to him and Ava. "I'll join yo-" I start to say but am cut off by Shelby. "Alright mister starter... how about a game of basketball?" she says holding out her game card.

"I was just thinking about how I didn't get enough shots up tonight... You ready to lose?" I respond with the most confidence I have shown all night. I succeed in making her laugh. "Says the guy about to get his butt whooped by a girl... on crutches!" she jokes back at me.

"Lead the way. If you can hobble all the way there, that is." I joke with a risky one. Hopefully she's not sensitive and can take a joke.

She laughs like I just hit my stride on my stand-up comedy special. Almost too much for as funny as I thought that joke was, but I am relieved and laugh along with her. "Wow, okay! Follow me, I have gotten pretty good at hobbling since I got hurt."

She does just that and I follow her to the arcade basketball game where she promptly leans her crutches up against the side of the game and stands in front of it, careful not to put too much weight on her bad leg. The game has two baskets side by side with enough room for two players to stand side by side in front of them. After swiping your card, you get 60 seconds to shoot as many times as you can. Whoever makes more obviously comes out the winner.

"Shall we?" I say, extending my game card. She nods to me, and I make the transaction, starting the game. Throughout the 60 seconds, I go as fast as I can. I chuck shot after sloppy shot up, many of them completely missing, all for me to look at my score of 47 at the end.

I look over at Shelby's score, hoping I have done enough to outdo her. She gives me a sort of 'take that' grin as I see the number 62 displaying her score.

"Woah, seriously? Over a shot made per second?" I say, shook by the result. "Don't sound so surprised. You may have been playing for a little bit now, but don't forget, I have been training my whole life." She tells me with a chip on her shoulder.

I look at her cast on her leg. To think she has put her whole life into this game... and now her season is getting stripped away from her from just an accident. How is she able to keep her smile? Her friendly attitude? When you think about how one injury could keep her from being able to play in college... being happy must be a daunting task for her.

"Well, you've got talent. No doubt about that." I tell her before asking. "Are you okay? ... I mean, with not being able to play this season... it must be hard."

She looks at me with softer eyes than she did before, like she is trying to pick her words carefully. "Well, it isn't easy I suppose, but no one promised us life would be easy. Loss can be hard, Rick... I uh... I know that you know that... but it's important to remember what you lose is part of a plan, and the void left behind can be filled again."

That was... profoundly deep to spring out at an arcade out of the blue. Not sure I like that she turned my question around on me, but I think she was just trying to help. This still gives me something to think about.

"Oh yeah? And who's plan would that be?" I ask her. She opens her mouth to answer, but before she can we are interrupted by Wyatt and Ava who rejoin us.

"Bro, you got beat by a girl?" Wyatt says chuckling.

"He says that like I didn't just get done beating him at skiball." Ava adds stopping Wyatt's chuckle dead in its tracks. "You weren't supposed to tell them!"

"Alright, I just need to run to the bathroom real fast, then we can go." Shelby tells us and heads off to the bathroom. Wyatt turns to us and says "I better go get the car warmed up... meet me out there in 5?"

We nod and he walks outside. Ava and I stand in awkward silence for a moment before she asks "Sooo... what did you think?"

I answer back quickly "Not bad at all! Wish we would have got thin crust though."

"Not the pizza, you numbskull! What do you think of Shelby?"

"Woah! I think numbskull is a little out of line!"

"You're right, too far... Now spit it out! What did you think?"

"Why should I have any thoughts? It's not like this was a date."

"You're two single people playing arcade games together all night. I am sure you have some thoughts about her."

"I mean... well" I try to pick my words so that I don't embarrass myself. "Yeah, she's cool... easy to joke around with."

"Pretty too, huh?"

"C'mon, stop that." I tell her as I see Shelby approaching us again out of the corner of my eye. Hopefully it wasn't obvious we were talking about her. As we are now all regrouped we decide to head out to the parking lot to meet up with Wyatt who is supposed to be waiting on us.

Opening the door to the arcade a cold gust of wind hits me. It continues to chill my cheek bones as I hold the door open for the ladies who follow me out.

Something else hits me as we enter the cold outdoors... Music, right in my ears. I turn my head to the direction the music is coming from. I see my friend Wyatt standing out in the cold with the back of his van propped open. The music coming from inside the van is playing loudly enough to fill the mostly otherwise quiet parking lot.

It isn't his normal, more obnoxious rap music he's blaring, however. No, this is more soft, older. Not necessarily my cup of tea, but... soothing. The song pairs well with the darkness of the night sky, and the few streetlights here work like candles to set the relaxing tone of this classical music.

Ava perks up as the song hits her ears and things start to make sense. This isn't something Wyatt would like, no, but her? This is right up her ally. As we get closer to him, he holds out his hand to Ava "My lady?" he says, asking her to dance by sticking to the classy character he has chosen to play tonight.

With the cold night I can't seem to tell what is wind burn and what is blush on Ava's cheeks as she takes Wyatts hand. "Well, how could I say no?"

"Easy, tell him 38 degrees is no time of year for an outdoor ball." I say, putting my two cents in.

"Dude!" Wyatt rebuttals at me for killing the mood... but I can tell I didn't do too much harm by the smile that remains on Ava's face. Besides, he needed someone to call out how cheesy this is.

"Fine, fine. I'll be quiet." I yield.

The two then start to slow dance under the night sky. As cheesy as it is, it seems to be working on Ava. His way of making it up to her for his lack of time spent with her lately, I'm sure.

Only problem is now that leaves me and Shelby awkwardly standing here together watching them dance. There's no chance that we're going to join in on the dancing, so I take a seat on the back of Wyatts van.

Shelby comes to join me and sits next to me. We don't really talk. We just sit there and enjoy being cold and listening to some good music together.

CHAPTER 9

First Game

The sound of muffled hype music coming from the gym fills our crowded locker room. We are all gathered for the first game of the season and even the seniors seem to be nervous. For good reason, too.

We're playing the Aurora Valley Water Snakes, a team that won districts just last year. With our own line up so drastically different than it was last year, it feels like the whole school is waiting to see if we will even be a team worth watching. A crushing defeat at home court in front of all our peers is what everyone in this locker room is trying to avoid.

AJ keeps pacing the room. Back and forth and back and forth. At this rate his legs will be burnt out before the game even starts.

"Yo, freshman. Quit acting so nervous. This is what you wanted, isn't it?" Matt calls over to AJ.

"Nervous? Me? No, no, I'm fine, I'm fine." AJ says back. Being a freshman that young about to go out and play in front of your whole school can be a scary feeling, especially in a game we're picked to lose. I remember the butterflies in my own belly my freshman year of track.

Matt calls AJ over to him. "Get over here and grab a seat. Try and relax. You'll be doing plenty of running up and down in just a few minutes."

He's right. I think we can win this game but it's going to take all of us playing our butts off to get it done. I hope we're all in the physical shape we need to be to play intense ball for an entire game.

I walk over to the corner of the locker room, where we have a toilet and sink tucked away. Above that sink is a mirror that I take a deep look into.

I haven't gotten a chance to see how I look with my full uniform on yet. I have on our white home jersey with STAGS written in brown letters on the chest just above my number, 36. The shoulders are also brown to add an offset to all the white. The shorts are white with the words WEST DES MOINES wrapping around the right pantleg in brown. I stair myself in my own green eyes, and look my black hair pull up so it doesn't fall in my eyes. If you had asked me a year ago, I never would have guessed I'd be where I am today.

"Alright everyone, bring it in!" I hear Coach Morgan enter the locker room and walk around the corner to regroup with the team.

We all gather around him for his pregame speech. "Alright gentleman, we can win here tonight... but it's not going to be easy. They ain't going to hand it to us. I know last year a lot of games we would count on John to do a lot of the heavy lifting. However, this team has big front court players. Forcing it in the paint is not our best option. I want our shooters to take shots. MAKE SURE THEY ARE CLEAN SHOTS MIND YOU... but take shots. Wyatt, you got a great 3 ball, I wanna see you use it tonight... Oh, and trust our point guard. If Rick makes a call out there, trust he sees something you don't. Get open and let him hit you on a pass... Alright John, break 'em down and let's get out there."

John puts out his arm, sending a signal for us to put our hands in as well. "Alright everyone, get in here." he shouts as we all pile our hands on top of one another. "STAGS ON 3 ... 1, 2, 3" he yells. "STAGS!!" we yell back complying to his instructions.

We then walk out of the locker room in a single file line. John leads the way with Matt following close behind him. After exiting the locker room, we enter a hallway that leads to the gym. The white block walls of the hall are littered with corny quotes the school painted on.

Things like 'The best view comes after the hardest climb' and 'A smooth sea never made a skilled sailor'. Well, even though the painted-on quotes failed at their goal of hyping me up, I have been preparing for a hard climb for a while now. Months and months of late nights in the driveway, and staying late after practice... I need to show everyone that Rick Joseph has more to offer than just 'the kid that did track.'

I take a deep breath in as we approach the double doors leading into the gym. I hear the chatter and cheers of all the fans inside already making themselves known loud and clear. As John Lynn enters, the room goes ballistic! 'I'm ready for this.' I think to myself, letting my breath out just before I enter the room myself.

We walk over to the side of the court where all our seats are waiting for us. I decide to take a fast scan around the crowd before I take my seat.

Sure enough, I see Ava and Shelby in the front row of the student section on the right side of the bleachers. A lot of the students showed up for the game. Some of them raise up cardboard cutouts of the faces of our senior captains, John and Matt.

Taking a quick peak over to the left side of the stands, I am able to spot my mom in the upper left. She is looking back at me, and we share a smile. Before I turn my head back to the court, I spot another face I just barely recognize, though it takes me a moment to place it. Sitting a few rows in front of my mom is the blonde headed girl from my dad's funeral, the one involved in his wreck. I clench my jaw in frustration at the memory seeing her brings about.

What is she doing here anyway? Does she know someone on the team? She said she wanted to be there for my family now. Is she here for me? No, I can't drive myself crazy with questions, not now. It will just throw off my game. I didn't work this hard to blow it now.

"All rise for the national anthem." We hear the announcer say over the intercom. We stand, face the flag on the right side of the room, and place our hands over our hearts.

As our country's theme song plays, I notice I happen to have a view of Aurora Valley's players in sight. They're big. Bigger than we are, for sure. Their average player's height is at least 6 feet, making our team look dwarfed in comparison.

Me doing any work in the paint is going to be a tall order but I can jump high on my lay ups and get something in off the glass. I'm just going to have to be smart about the way I play this.

The anthem ends and we take our spots on the court. John Lynn is in the middle, ready to jump for the ball. He is lined up across from a guy who is maybe an inch taller than him, but with not nearly as much muscle on his frame.

To the left of John is Matt with his eyes glued to where the action is about to take place. To the right of him is AJ, and behind is me and Wyatt. I take a glance at the other team's point guard that will be on me all game. Tall and skinny. He has a head band on to keep his long hair out of his eyes, and a t-shirt under his jersey.

No way of telling how athletic he is until I see him move. However, I bet if I am shifty enough, I can blow by this guy. The referee starts making his way to the center of the court with the game ball in hand. John and the other team's center are already there, ready to jump.

My stomach jumps into my throat as the pre-game jitters are in full effect. The crowd seems spilt on if they should stay quiet for the jump ball or cheer louder. The student section seems decided as their roaring chants fill the gym.

I dig my feet into the gym floor in my stance. I'm ready to take off running in the direction of the outcome of this jump ball. I look over to Wyatt to see if he is ready and he gives me a nod as if to say, 'Let's do this.' He's a hard guy to shake but he has been quiet most of the day, letting me know he must be feeling the pressure at least a little bit.

The referee takes the ball and holds it underhanded in between the two big men. With his whistle in his mouth, he tosses the ball as straight as he can in the air and takes a step back quickly.

The ball hangs in the air for what feels like an hour in my anticipation that the ball might come my way. In actuality, it takes only a few seconds for John to jump up forward and high using his big body to gain an edge over the defender. He ends up being able to slap the ball in our direction.

It doesn't come directly to me. Instead, it hits the ground slightly to my left. I sprint to it quickly and grab it before it gets too far away. I start dribbling just a few feet back from half court and make my assessment of the defense.

John has already made his way into the paint, trying to get open. Their center is covering him hard. Matt and AJ are covered more loosely. However, not by much. They are still being kept from making their way closer to the basket or having any shot at a 3 pointer. We're going to have to find a way to make space somewhere.

Wyatt moves himself near the left wing on the 3-point line. Just as I cross half court, the other teams point guard steps up to guard me. I start to move to the left side of the court. I have to dribble with my left hand as now the defender is almost glued to my right shoulder, not wanting me to make my way closer to the basket.

He's the only one on his team playing defense this tight, and I am about to make him pay for it. I dribble the ball behind my back switching it to my right hand. I proceed to take one hard step to the right, making it look like I am trying to change direction.

He bites and turns hard to the right to follow me. I cross the ball back over, this time in front of my body. Now with the ball back in my left hand, I speed past him faster than my opponent can change direction.

Still, I will never make it all the way in for a layup or dunk. Not with the other team's center camped under the basket. The best I could hope for is a fast mid-range shot, but that's not really what I'm after.

Now I am freely running toward the rim on the left side. This causes the defender on Wyatt to pull off and try to stop me, just like I was planning. I pick up the ball and hook it over my left shoulder. I pass it just over the other teams shooting guard, and right into the hands of Wyatt.

Wyatt takes his opening and nails the jump shot putting us up by 3. Our home crowd begins to cheer. The announcer calls out "3-point shot made by number 0, Herbert. Off the assist by number 36, Joseph."

Now it's time to see how well we can do on defense. The other team's center throws the ball in, passing it to their point guard. Before I can step up to guard him, the ball is already out of his hands. He makes a pass to the small forward who is being loosely covered by AJ. It's all too easy for him to make AJ pay for the relaxed defense as he drives in on him and hits the layup.

"Martenez! Step up to the plate and play some defense! Let's go!" Coach Morgan yells, upset to have to give up those points.

John throws in the ball to me from the side line and play resumes. I jog it down the court and run over to the right wing. I scan my options. This would be a hard shot for me, so I pass it to Matt who is at the top of the key.

Matt fakes the 3 right away causing the kid guarding him to jump. Matt dribbles right by him and as he enters the paint he fakes a pass to John. This causes the other team's center to put all his focus on John for a moment. Just a moment, but long enough for Matt to jump up and dunk it in for 2 points.

That really puts the fans on their feet. The cheers get so loud it's getting hard to hear Coach. Too bad it doesn't last long, as our opponents answer back with a 3-point shot of their own. This time, it was my fault. I thought my defense was good, but I need to stay closer to the other team's point guard to make up for the height difference.

We're now tied up at 5 points each in just the first few plays of the first quarter. I can already tell this is going to be a grueling game. We go back and forth for the rest of the first half.

With just seconds left of the second quarter, John jumps up and hits a violent block over the other team's power forward as he tries to drive in. The ball makes its way to Matt who hits me on a pass. With nothing but clear court in front of me, I sprint down to the basket. No one is able to catch me.

I pick the ball up as I get close, take my gather step, and leap into the air. I had a lot of momentum behind the jump, and it does just the trick to give me the height I need to two hand slam the ball in.

The half time whistle blows, and the announcer calls out "That's the end of the first half. The West Des Moine Stags lead the Aurora Valley Water Snakes 34-31 in a good first half of play.

Meanwhile, I take in the feeling of the adoring crowd. I enjoy the accomplishment of my first real in-game points. Amongst the cheers, I can pick out my mom's voice. It brings a smile to my face.

We all huddle up to the side of the court around Coach Morgan as the other team does the same with their own Coach. Coach begins his half time speech about how we are playing great, but the second half won't be easy.

He can tell we are all tired and have been going all out trying to keep this lead. He draws up some plays on his clipboard for us to try if we find ourselves in a tight spot. Before we know it, the whistle blows and it's time to start playing again. All of us only have our breath half caught as we return to the court.

The Water Snakes start the 3rd quarter off with the ball. Their point guard hits their power forward on a cut who is then able to capitalize on the pass and hit a mid-range jumper. This effectively cuts our lead to just one point.

We attempt to answer back, but a missed 3-pointer by Matt puts the ball right back into the Water Snakes hands. This gives them the chance to get another 2 points and take our lead.

This time, however, I am able to return the favor with a jump shot from the free throw line. The ball makes it in, giving us back our 1-point lead. From there, the lead changes are many. Neither team is able to add to their lead enough to get more than a 1- or 2-point advantage. That kind of back-and-forth play is exciting for both teams. Being on the court, you can almost hear the pants and gasps for air more than the conversion of the crowd. Nevertheless, we all just have to tough it out. The game is too close to send in the subs; we need our best player on the court to win it. John forces his way in for a layup, making the score 50-49 with us taking the lead.

With just 1:30 left in the game, we all hope that will be the last lead change. The other team in bounds the ball and play starts. The point guard that I am guarding walks the ball down the court slowly, clearly trying to take time off the clock.

Soon enough though, he starts jogging to the right wing of the court. I stick to him hard, not giving him any room. I am completely focused on him. Too much so, even, because before I know it, I run into a brick wall of a screen set by the Water Snakes' shooting guard.

It doesn't make me fall but it definitely makes me stumble. This makes me powerless as I have to sit there and watch them take an open 3 point shot. It feels like I am being kicked in the chest as I watch the ball go in, giving them a 50-52 lead.

We likely will have just one more chance to score, and if we don't get a 3… it's overtime. Looking at my team around me, I can see Wyatt and AJ with their hands on their knees panting. It's clear we need to win this now for our best shot at avoiding wearing ourselves out any farther in an overtime match.

The clock is ticking. This time, John throws the ball in to Wyatt. This decision makes sense because Wyatt is our best shot to make a 3. However, when we get down the court, it's clear the other team isn't going to let him shoot.

Wyatt tries to put some moves on them to get open, but it's no good. The Water Snakes are not going to let him have it. He tries to look for AJ, who also made a 3 in the 2nd quarter, but he is locked down as well.

I start trying to get open. I fake like I am cutting inside to attempt to tie it with a 2-point. I make a quick cut back at the free throw line and return to the top of the key, getting open in the process.

Wyatt is so locked up, even passing is difficult. He lobs the pass high in the air to get it over the waving arms of his opponent. I jump up and catch the pass above my head.

No one is open and my only option is to shoot now. If I try to drive in, I risk losing an open shot. Shooting this deep isn't my specialty, but no one can deny it's the best course of action to win this game.

I don't have all the time in the world as the other team's point guard is correcting and making his way over to me. I have to do this now, no time to debate it. I line up my shot and jump, extending my arms and flicking my wrist as I release my shot.

The ball flies on a straight path all the way to the rim. It hits the back of the rim and bounces up. I wait in limbo for the ball to come down as there is still a chance it will go in.

Every basketball movie I have ever watched has told me that the last shot happens in slow motion, but it doesn't feel that way. In reality, it feels like your brain is working at super speed thinking of all the possibilities and outcomes that could be.

In the end, no matter how fast you think, you can't slow down time. It only takes seconds to watch as the ball hits the front of the rim and bounces out. My last shot just lost us the game and it's too little too late to do anything about it.

The other team grabs the ball and are able to hold on to it for the last few seconds. The game ends in our defeat. I keep my head down, not daring to look into the stands at the schools reaction to me blowing the game.

"It's alright, man." a clearly sad Wyatt comes up to me.

"Alright?" an angry John joins the conversation. "It's not alright. You cost us the game." He says, throwing his hands up before stomping away. The sad thing about it is... I can't help but agree with him.

I notice Coach Morgan making his way over to me. I brace myself for the butt chewing I am sure I am about to get. He towers over me in his brown sweat suit. "Well, I think we need to work on your 3-point shot." He says "But do NOT beat yourself up over this. That is the nature of the game. If you would have made that shot, we would all be throwing you up on our shoulders. That's basketball for you. I've seen and played my fair share of it, and I wouldn't have done anything different than you did."

I look up at him. "So you're not going to bench me?"

"No, I am not going to bench you. You played hard tonight, and you play hard in practice. That's what I am looking for. It's because of that, I know you'll keep improving. That's all a coach can ask for."

His words give me some comfort. However, the pain of a 0-1 start to the season makes me wince internally with how close we were to being 1-0 every time it crosses my mind.

I make my way to a dead silent locker room to grab my bag. Everyone is most likely just sad about the loss, I try to reassure myself. However, I can't help but feel like they are quiet because they can't stand the sight of me.

I grab my bag, throw my basketball shoes inside, and slip on my slides to replace them. I then throw my bag over my shoulder and make my retreat. Fleeing from the negative energy that seems to be aimed in my direction.

I meet my mom near the front door of the school to catch my ride home. As I approach her, she gives her expected "HEY! You played so good out there!" I know she means well, but I don't intend to stay in the school any longer tonight. "Thanks." I say as I keep walking towards the door, hoping she will follow me through the exit.

"Rick, Violet!" a female voice calls out before we go through the door. I hope it isn't who I think it is, but I turn to in fact see the face of the lady from the funeral. "I just wanted to catch you and say great job tonight." She says.

So she did just come to watch me. What is her problem? Does she not find this weird? Maybe she's vindictive and has now made it her goal to see every low moment in my life. No, as mad as I am, even I can tell that my thoughts are becoming irrational. I better try to cool down and get out of this place.

"Um...thanks." I mutter, trying to make it clear I don't want to talk. Instead of breaking off the talk, she makes a statement. "My name is Nicole, by the way... I hope to catch more of your games this season!"

"Oh... cool." I say back to her.

It's at this point I think she gets the hint that I want her to go. She bids us a good night and we go out on our own ways.

I try to not to work myself up too much. All I can think about is getting back to work at improving my game tomorrow.

CHAPTER 10

Reconciliation

Tuesday. The next day. Sleeping last night turned out to be more difficult a task than I would have liked. Every time I got close to drifting off and letting myself relax, my eyes would shoot open with the feeling of abrupt anger. That caused the twitching flex of every muscle in my body.

My drowsy brain mixed with my sore legs from playing almost the full game without a sub has a noticeable impact on my mood today at school. Walking the hallways, I get more and more frustrated. My own blend of narcissism and paranoia convinces me that every wandering eye that looks in my direction is judging me for losing the game last night.

I tell myself that's crazy talk. In reality, why would most of the school really care if we lost or not. Nobody is really a superfan of high school sports after all. They likely wouldn't even care as much as if their favorite professional team lost. Still though, crazy or not, this feeling of being judged lives in the pit of my chest. And to be honest, it's pissing me off.

I NEED to show them. When I lead us to a championship, they will all look at me differently. The worth in myself that only I know, will turn into common knowledge, and the respect I deserve will be handed to me.

Despite all odds, I drag myself halfway through the school day and somehow make it to lunch. The traffic in the room is busy as per usual. Teenagers take their seats at round tables that hold 6 each. At the table I sit at, we only need 3. I take my seat next to Wyatt and Ava, who have already made their way through the lunch line.

As they work on eating their school pizza, (that in my opinion closer resembles cardboard than the Italian cuisine) I pull out my lunch that I packed at home. A ham and Swiss cheese sandwich with chips and an apple.

"Hey bro." Wyatt greets me. I nod back at him. "How's it going?" He asks.

"I've been better." I tell him. He tilts his head in confusion "You're not still upset about last night, are you?" he asks.

"How could I not be? It's only been one night. I think I am still a reasonable amount of upset about losing the game for us."

"Nah man. Overall, both of our stat lines were pretty good. Besides, we got plenty more chances to win games."

"You don't get it, man. Colleges only care about stat lines if you can show that they translate to winning games. If you can't help their team win, they don't care about you at all. Falling short when the game was on the line last night just makes everyone think I can't be counted on."

Wyatt shakes his head at me. I can even tell by Ava's body language that's she's cringing a bit as well. Wyatt gets honest with me. "Bro, you need to relax. Yes, winning is great and we should try our best to get the dub, but you're being a bit dramatic about the loss this time around."

I shake my head in response to his accusation as I angrily start to bite into my lunch. I don't engage in what Wyatt and Ava are sharing in for the rest of our lunch break. I am forced to think about that fact that Wyatt is right about how moody I'm acting.

The problem is that I don't care. Sure, I could put on a smile and be happy go lucky, but I am angry. I've spent so much time already trying to hide my sadness about the loss of my father this year. Frankly, I feel letting my frustration show is within my right.

The school day carries on until its finally time for the one thing that will make me feel happier right now. Practice. Lacing up my shoes for my warmup before things get going feels like opening the door from behind the bars of a cell that holds me, along with all the other frustrating things in the world. Continuing to walk out of it and into the true freedom that is hard work.

I start to shoot around with my teammates while we all wait on Coach to arrive. I focus most of my shots on the 3-point line, doing my best to improve from that range.

John Lynn takes his place at the free throw line as that is clearly an area that he would like to improve on. Even in this close proximity, he doesn't even look my way. He seems down or stressed. Between Matt and AJ joking around on the other side of the court, and my lunch conversation with Wyatt, it seems John might be the only one taking this loss as hard as me.

Just then, the door to the gym burst open. I turn to look, expecting to see Coach. To my surprise, it's not him, but instead it's someone I don't recognize. He's tall, but pretty slender, wearing a ball cap and a dirty hoodie and jeans.

Dirty isn't unusual in Iowa, however. We have a strong community of construction workers and farmers. So we don't view it as unclassy. Rather a sign that he most likely took a break from hard labor to be here.

"Dad?" John Lynn says, in a state of confusion. It's odd for a parent to show up here, these are closed practices after all. John Lynn's dad starts to talk "Hey, son. I thought I'd sit in on practice tonight after watching last night's game. It brought me to the conclusion that you must not be practicing hard enough." He ends his statement with attitude in his voice.

John starts to look more and more uncomfortable "Dad, please just go back home. You're not supposed to be here."

John's dad whips his head sternly at the response from John and tension fills the room. As he starts a march towards John, he says "I didn't come all the way here for you give me lip, boy!". At this point, I'm sure everyone is wondering if we should step in, though our youth and lack of experience keeps all of us from pulling the trigger on helping John out.

As his dad gets closer to him, I start to notice the size difference between the two. Yeah, John's dad is tall, but John is a big lineman and carries a lot more muscle than his dad. John's body language says it all as he brings his shoulders in and puts his head down. It's clear that despite being the bigger guy... John is scared of his father.

"No, I came here to make sure you don't embarrass me again like you did last night." John's father tells him, now just inches from his face.

From the corner of my eye, I see Matt slowly walking towards the pair. He's moving slow and looking nervous. He probably doesn't know what he's going to say when he gets there, but as the only other senior in the group he must think it falls on him to stop whatever it is that we are witnessing here.

"MR. LYNN, IS THERE SOMETHING I CAN HELP YOU WITH?" A voice that isn't Matt's calls from the tunnel to the relief of all of us in the room. I turn my head to see Coach Morgan finally arriving on the scene. I don't think I have ever been so happy to see that bright colored track suit of his.

"There's something you can help my son with... it's called a free throw." Mr. Lynn responds, not backing down like I hoped he would when another adult entered the room.

"If you want your son to keep improving, we need to have practice. Which is not open to the parents. So, if that's all you had to say, then its time for you to go." Coach tells him, keeping his cool throughout.

John's dad throws up his hands "Fine! Have it your way. I'll be heading out." He turns to look at John before he starts walking away. "John, be sure to do some improving tonight." He says before leaving the school.

"Alright everyone, line up for drills. We have a lot to go over tonight." Coach yells out trying to proceed with business as usual. Everyone slowly starts to shake off the awkwardness of the encounter as practice goes on. Everyone other than John, who moves slow and appears down all night.

In fact, he seems closer to walking off the court and heading home than he does to putting in effort to get better. It's clear his dad rattled him. I hope he's able to bounce back and things don't just get worse for him when he gets home later. That kind of pressure must be hard to live with. The make believe pressure that put on myself, seems to have a living body and face within Johns life.

CHAPTER 11

Shooters Shoot

After practice is all wrapped up for the night, I decide to stay late. Wyatt doesn't stay with me this evening. He said something about how Ava has been missing him with all the time he's been spending practicing lately. He's normally my ride back home when I stay late, so my mom is going to have to pick me up in an hour or so.

I normally don't like having to bug her, but this is important. I just need to get this 3-point shot down. If I can get this missing piece of the puzzle fixed, I think I'll feel more like a complete player.

I take aim from the top of the key wondering at what point in my jump I should release the ball. I think about how much power I should put into my shot. I jump, shooting the ball on my way up into the air. I let go of it in front of my face with a good amount of force. It flies through the air hitting the backboard and rolling down the right side of the basket without hitting the rim.

I shake my head as I walk to get the ball, knowing I'm in for a rough night going by that first shot. "Try putting some more arch on it." I hear Shelbys voice. "You are shooting it on a line like a sniper rifle. It's a little less controlled and easy to overshoot that way."

"What are you still doing here?" I ask her, trying to decide if I am happy to see her or mad that she's giving me critiques.

"I have been staying for girls practice even though I can't play. I saw you in here as I was walking by and thought I'd see why you're still here so late." She tells me.

"That much should be obvious." I say to her in a down and hanging my head kind of tone. "I need to improve. If I can't be relied on to shoot in the late stages of the game... I may as well not be on the court at all."

She gives me a similar look to the one Wyatt and Ava gave me earlier at the lunch table. One that gives me the impression I may be being an ever so slightly amount of a drama queen. In truth, I can't tell yet if it hurts me that my friends don't get how I feel about myself in this moment, or if little by little it is starting to make me feel like my problems aren't as big as I am building them up to be.

"I don't think that's true Rick." Shelby says. "I watched your game. You were playing tough defense throughout. You handled the ball well, and even though you missed that shot, you did have some points. Basketball is a team effort; you can't blame losing the game on one missed shot."

"What would you recommend I do, then? Just rely on my defense and passing to get me to a d1 level?"

"No, I actually think your hard work after practice is great! Afterall, no one has gotten better at something by not doing it."

"Great! Then I don't get the problem."

She takes a pause before responding and looks me right in my eyes. "I just don't know if you're here for the right reasons..." She says. I raise my eyebrows and exhale. Not sure if I am ready for the conversation I worry she is steering towards. "Rick, it's no secret that you've had... just about as hard a year as anyone could have. I'm just worried you're pouring all this time into your game... to try and fill something that's missing."

I instantly think that's she's wrong. This is just about basketball... right? Still, I can see why she could come to that conclusion, I suppose. Sure, I trained very hard to get to the level I got to in track, but the attitude... it was clearly different. I was never this brooding.

Basketball started out so fun, it was the bright spot of my day. Somehow it seems I have managed to turn it into the same color of gray as the rest of my life over time.

Shelby keeps talking "I want you to know I am your friend. You can come to me with more than just shooting help. You can come to me with life help."

Life help? Honestly, as nice as she is, I don't believe she can help me much, if at all, in life. I don't know if anyone can. "Just shooting help is all I need!" I say in a cheerier tone, trying to change the mood of the room. "If you don't mind, I need to get back to it." I say, now trying to end our chat.

I once again line up a shot as Shelby stands by and watches me. I take the shot and this time hit the front of the rim hard, sending the ball bouncing back quickly. I grit my teeth as I watch it bounce right to Shelby.

"Try flicking your wrist more. Like this" she says, picking up the ball. Then, from the left side of the top of the key, she lines up and takes her shot. She's careful not to jump so she doesn't hurt her knee. The ball takes a beautiful arching path before going straight through the rim, hitting nothing but the net.

Hard to argue with her pointers after seeing her results. 'What I would give to have that kind of accuracy' I think to myself. Shelby puts her hands on her hips and gives a cocky grin. I can feel my face go flush with embarrassment after her witnessing me struggle with something that seems so easy to her.

"Show off." I say with an awkward chuckle to hide the insecurity I am feeling while also trying to let her know that I am in fact impressed. Then she cheerfully asks "If you want, I could help coach you after practices. We could get your jump looking clean in no time!"

I consider it briefly before answering, but in the end, I have to put pride aside. This one is a no brainer if I am truly serious about getting better. Which I am. "Really?! You would be willing to do that?"

"Well, I can't play right now anyway. I figure I will become a coach at some point in my life, why not have you be my first student?" she says.

"Well, how could I say no?" I say, letting her know I am happy to have the help. However, as the question leaves my lips, I notice her smile soften a touch. She takes a deep inhale like she is gearing up to tell me there's a catch.

"Well," she says, "There's a catch."

I knew it. There's no way someone would want to stay an hour after practice each day to watch a sport an injury is preventing them from being able to play if they are not getting anything out of the deal. "Alright." I say. "Name it."

"I'll help you every day, but Wednesdays." She tells me. "On Wednesdays, you are going to come to youth group at my church with me." She says it like I don't have any choice in the matter.

"Church? What does that have to do with basketball?" I ask.

"More than you might think. I believe your walk with Jesus effects every part of your life."

"I'm not against it. I've just never been before. I might be a little... out of place." I say, hoping once she knows that I have no clue how to even act in church, she'll realize I won't fit in and drop the conversation.

"Trust me, no one is out of place there. All are welcome." She says. I doubt it. However, my lack of knowledge on the subject leaves me unable to come up with a good reason to object. "Come on, what could it hurt?" asks Shelby. "Worst case scenario, you get shooting lessons from the best shooter in the state."

She brags, giving herself a pat on the back. "Best case... you get some of those demons off your back as well."

Like I said, I know nothing about religion, so I don't know if she's being metaphorical or if she is crazy enough to think that there are actual demons on my back. Still, there is one think I do know, and that is the fact that she has the shooting abilities I want. She also has the basketball knowledge of how to teach that ability to me.

Although I am sceptic on how going to church could improve my mood, the chance it could really make me feel less... down, is inciting. It would be nice to feel good for a change. So, without any better plan, I accept her offer. Looks like I am heading to church.

CHAPTER 12

A Place to Fit In

It just so happens that the next day was a Wednesday. That meant it was time for me to hold up my end of the bargain I made with Shelby. After a hard practice, I was supposed to meet Shelby by the front door of the school.

She has a car and is giving me a ride to youth group rather than having me meet her there. I don't remember what her parents do exactly, but everyone talks about how they're loaded, so it wasn't a surprise when Wyatt and Ava told me that nice sports car I see in senior parking every day belonged to her.

With my sweats on, I stand by the door waiting for her to get out of girl's practice. However, I am taken by surprise when John Lynn seems to spawn out of nowhere, also in his sweats. He sets his backpack on the floor and leans against the wall opposite the side I am standing on.

It seems understood that we aren't going to do the whole 'small talk' dance. I mean, what would that even look like? 'Sorry your dad is a jerk, but at least you have one, right?' Yeah, no thanks.

Instead, we both pull out our phones and act too busy to talk. The only problem with that is our school is notorious amongst us kids for not having good enough service to access games or internet. That means unless he's typing a novel to someone in his text, I know that we're both just pretending to be glued to our screens.

I know John drives a truck, so unless it's broken down, I don't know why he is waiting at all. Maybe he's going out with some friends tonight and he's waiting on them to show up.

After waiting the longest five minutes and forty seconds of my life, (I know because I was just staring at my clock on my phone the whole time.) Shelby finally comes around the corner.

She's in jeans and a brown hoodie that says 'LADY STAGS' on the chest, which is a name I really wish our school would have thought through better.

"Hey! You guys ready?" She greets us with her classic upbeat attitude. John and I glance at each other with puzzled faces as we start to put together that she was talking to both of us.

"Oh yeah, I forgot to tell you… Rick is coming along with us this time. hope that's not a problem." She says, walking past John like she doesn't actually care if he has a problem with it at all.

If anyone has a problem with her not letting them know about this situation, it should be me. At this point though, what can I do? Tell her I don't want John to go to church with us? How much of a jerk would that make me?

Besides, with what I saw the other night, he might need a 'divine intervention' just as much as I do. We both shrug our shoulders in acceptance that this is happening. "Nah, it's cool." John claims, despite his tone sounding less than 'cool.'

We quickly hit our first obstacle of the night when we get to Shelby's car. Like I said, it's a sports car. If you've ever seen a back seat in a sport car, you know that leg room is pretty much non-existent.

With this in mind, I call out "shotgun." on our way to the car. That being my first word uttered of the night probably makes me sound like a dork I realize after saying it.

"Uh... no, man. I can't fit back there. Besides, you're like 5 feet. It makes more sense for you to ride in the back." John tells me. The short joke seemed unneeded to me, but he had a point.

Not wanting to be the cause of conflict this early in the night, especially in front of Shelby, I agree to take the back seat. I cram in and we start on our way.

The inside of the car is nice and well kept. Although, even being shorter than John, my knees are brushing against the seat in front of me. Along the trip, I wonder how Shelby got John to agree to come to church with her. He doesn't just jump out at me as the 'holy' type.

She probably just had to invite him, I doubt he would turn down the chance to hang out with a pretty girl. That is likely the reason he is riding with us when he has his own truck and is capable of driving himself.

Still, after what I saw the other day, there's an equal chance that he would take any reason not to be at his house longer than he has to.

Soon, the short drive concludes, and we make it to the church. The building seems to be the size of a small school. A decent number of cars are parked in the parking lot, but nothing too crazy. After climbing my way out of the backseat, we make our way inside.

We take a right at the entry doors into a classroom full of various kids all around our same age. Chairs are all in lines pointing towards the front of the room. Soft Christian music plays to fill the room with some background noise. Not that it needs it so much, most the kids are having conversations, and everyone seems to be having a good time.

John grabs a seat while I take notice of the posters hanging around the room, most of them being some sort of cartoonish illustration with bible verses under them.

"Is that a new face I see?" I hear the voice of a rather cheerful man. "Yep! This is my friend Rick!" Shelby answers for me.

The man looks to be somewhere in his 40's. He's short with a buzz cut and a blonde beard with hints of red attached to it. He looks like an athlete, which I wasn't expecting. I guessed most pastors would be old, and likely out of shape. But this guy's arms look like they are about to bust out of his blue polo shirt. His green eyes look directly in mine as he reaches out to shake my hand.

"Nice to meet you, Rick! I'm Hugh Wilson and I'm the youth pastor here." He says, griping my hand with the force of a thousand men. "Nice to meet you." I reply trying not to cringe in pain.

"Well, first timer or main stayer, we like to make all feel welcome here. I am about to get my lesson started but come find me after and we'll get to know each other. We'd like to know more about you." He says, before heading to the front of the room. His exit gives Shelby and I a chance to take our seats next to John.

Although Mr. Hugh seemed like a nice guy, I doubt I'll be finding him to have a chat after service. It's nothing personal; I just normally like to slip out of places without making an ordeal of my exit. My focus is called back to the front of the room as the lights dim and music starts to turn up a little louder.

Everyone in the room rises to their feet, leaving me the only one sitting down. I take the hint and join my peers standing before I am noticed being different than the others. A projector begins to put the lyrics to a song called 'Our God is an Awesome God' on the wall that we are all facing.

I take a scan around the room looking to see how many people's mouths are moving. Being the same age as everyone here, I know that singing or doing anything else that would make you vulnerable to being criticized is very difficult to do. That is why it's so baffling to me when I notice how much of the room is singing along.

THE PATH THE BALL TAKES | 79

Sure, a few of them are mumbling the words, but a few of them are really SINGING like this is their audition for Broadway type of singing. I'll be honest, most of them wouldn't get the job. Some of the loudest voices filling the room are pitchy and unpleasant to the ear... but the smiles coming off those faces... it's like they couldn't possibly care less what they sound like.

I note it as intriguing and leave it as that for the time being. The song only lasts about 3 minutes. Afterward, we are all invited to retake our seats by Mr. Hugh as he takes center stage. "Alright everyone, tonight I have a lesson planed in the book of Daniel. If you have your Bible and want to follow along, I would think that's a good idea." He starts.

"When you think of Daniel, what is the first think that comes to mind?" He asks. I of course have no idea who Daniel is, so I keep my lips shut. It doesn't take long before some girl in the front row calls out "The lion's den!"

Mr. Hugh gives a nod and a smile. "GOOD! Yes, I would say that likely is his most famous feat, one that undoubtedly required faith in the face of fear. When I ask everyone what they think of Daniel after my lesson tonight, I hope your answers will change to 'Someone that had faith in the face of fear'. See, yes, the lion's den seems like a very scary moment for Daniel, but we're going to go over his life and I'll show you that overcoming fear was a big theme for him throughout."

Now, as someone who has no clue about Daniel, and being a teenage boy... a story of a lion's den grabbed my attention. It instantly put an image in my head of a guy fighting lions in a gladiator arena. I think this Daniel guy must have been a strong fighter. I lean forward in my chair to hear about what other show of skills he performed in his life.

However, I realize about 10 minutes into Mr. Hugh's 45 minute long talk, that Daniel probably didn't fight anyone, not even the lions! As a matter of fact, I learn he got ripped from his home as a young man and had to face all sorts of hard times and that he was an old man at the time that he got thrown in the lion's den.

There was one thing that kept him going through it all... his commitment to Yahweh, or God. Hearing how hard his life was almost left me with more questions than answers. If it weren't for how Mr. Hugh wrapped up the talk, I likely would have left youth group thinking that the followers of Yahweh are cursed to have a hard life and that maybe the best thing to do would be just to avoid being thrown into my own metaphorical lion's den all together.

Before he finished though, he said something that changed how I looked at the whole ordeal. Daniel didn't trust or follow God because he thought He would keep him from having hard times, he did it because he knew God would get him through those hard times.

When I think about my own recent struggles, it still hurts to think about. Fear of losing a basketball game. Fear that I am not good enough. The struggle of growing up without a dad even. The last bit of my life has felt like the hardships will never end. I jump one hurtle just to be met with an even taller one on the other side.

Daniel, however, was met with a lifetime of hardships, and remained optimistic through it all. I think it's because he has something I don't. Even my moody behaver at school the last couple days. I fear I am wearing my scars everywhere I go. letting them make me a more a more angry, distrusting... and scared person. What Daniel had was different and I am not entirely sure how to get it. But I think... I think that I might want it.

CHAPTER 12.5

(Interlude) Wyatt's Story

Wyatt's van smelled of fast food and oiled rubber. He noticed while driving down the road to a local outdoor court. It was a rare day for this time of the year where it was bearable to play basketball outside, as long as you had a hoodie, of course.

Wyatt had hoped the aforementioned smell would cover up musk coming off the teenage athletes that he had riding with him. The smell of fast food was courtesy of a bag with greasy burger's remains brought in by, and now currently sitting at the feet of his front passenger seat, Matt Carder.

The smell of oiled rubber was from a box of new basketball shoes that AJ currently had his head inside, admiring. "Oh man! Let me tell you, if you guys think I'm hard to guard now, just wait until I got these bad boys on!" AJ brags from the backseat.

"Man, you really think some new kicks are going to make that much of a difference? You still won't be able to score on me, I can tell you that much." Matt says back.

"Besides, I thought we we're heading to the court to work on your defense, AJ?" Wyatt asks.

"Yeah, that's the plan. That doesn't mean I can't get a few buckets as well." AJ answers. AJ had explained to the boys that growing up, his family moved around a lot. Making it hard for him to acquire friends. This lead to a lot of days playing basketball alone. Which was great for shooting, but not so much for defense… as there was no one to defend against. AJ had talked Wyatt into picking him up this morning and bringing him to the mall to get these shoes that he was so convinced would make him a better player. AJ, being only a freshman, must have felt begging for a ride was his only option since he couldn't drive himself.

Matt had overheard them making plans at practice and asked to tag along. Wyatt was for sure taken back by Matt wanting to come. AJ made sense; he needed to use Wyatt for his car. Matt, however, had a car, and probably plenty of other friends to hang out with.

Choosing to hang out with people he didn't know well seemed odd. Then again, Matt was well liked by everyone and had lots of friends for a reason, Wyatt thought to himself. It's probably because he takes the time to hang out with new people.

Of course, Wyatt had other friends too, other than Ava and Rick. Though, if he was being honest, he couldn't remember the last time he hung out with any of them.

Soon, the court becomes so close it becomes visible. A sigh of disappointment lets out of the boys as they pull into the parking lot and realize that the court is packed.

One half of the court was taken over by some of the town's senior citizens that brought their own net to play pickle ball. That's always a sad sight for young hoopers to see. However, it didn't surprise Wyatt given the game's growth in popularity in their area. The other half of the court was taken by some guys playing a 2 on 2 game.

"Dang! We're never going get a game in." AJ sighs as they (now out of the car) approach the side of the court. This was one of the reasons why Wyatt preferred to play pickup games in Ricks driveway. The only thing he ever had to wait on there was for Mrs. Joseph to back her car out every once in a while.

"Nah man, we'll get on. Just might have to wait a second." Wyatt says, hoping to inspire hope that this wasn't a wasted trip.

"I ain't going to be waiting too long." Matt says, like he has something up his sleeve. "HEY FELLAS, WE GOT NEXT GAME." He calls out to the guys playing.

Wyatt was unsure of this strategy. For one, the guys looked older, and a little sketchy. They might not be the kind of guys that would take kindly to being ordered off the court. They were playing with a speaker on the side of them blasting rap music. Wyatt didn't mind; it was the same kind of music that he might use to get hype before a game.

He did, however, know boundaries and it was clear the older people on the pickle ball side of the court were not enjoying the profanity. Their dirty looks given to the guys playing were evidence to that.

About that time, one of the guys scored a mid-range bucket. As he takes the ball back to top of the key, he answers Matt "Next? Nah, we're going be playing a few more. You can play when we're done if you're still hanging around."

The man looked to still be in his 20's, as did the rest of his 3 friends playing with him. He was tall and dressed in baggy shorts. He wasn't wearing a shirt, revealing a slim but athletic build. This lack of clothing let Wyatt know they had probably been playing for a while. It was too cold to be without a shirt unless you were very warmed up. His white headband pulled back his shoulder length blonde hair.

AJ chimed into the dispute. "C'mon man we just want to get a practice game in."

"Your ears working, bro? I said we ain't going to be done for a while." The man snapped back as he checked the ball, and chest passed it to his teammate. To this response, AJ looked down, defeated, at his new pair of shoes, that he had yet to lace up, in his hands.

Matt looked as though he was ready to throw down and Wyatt wanted to avoid that. He would do what he had to for his friends, but he always fancied himself more of a talker than a fighter. He had to interject.

"He's right guys. Looks like these guys need more practice than we do anyway." He said, making sure it was so loud the guys on the court could hear him.

It was just like Wyatt. He couldn't help but throw out a witty remark, even in times where it can get him in trouble. Risky as it was, Wyatt knew baiting these guys with a challenge was their best chance of getting on the court.

Right on queue, one of the guys shoots a 3-pointer that hits the rim and bounces away. "See what I mean?" Wyatt says with a smirk. This earns him some laughs from Matt and AJ.

In most cases, playground insults wouldn't work. However, if Wyatt knew anything for sure, it's that hoopers never miss an opportunity to shut up trash talkers.

The man grabbed the ball and looked at his friends who met him with a shrug. He then said "Alright then man, you asked for it. You wanna be embarrassed so bad? Let's run the 3's"

Wyatt couldn't help but be proud of himself and how well his plan had worked. AJ got his shoes on, and the 3 boys took the court. One of the guys in the other group agreed to sit out and watch so there could be even teams of 3.

"What are we playing to?" Wyatt asked.

"First to 3 makes. Any make counts as 1." One of the team members answered. This would be a short and sweet game, very little room for error.

"Oh, and by the way, it's make it, take it. Since you were so cocky, I'm gonna be nice enough to give you ball first. It'll be the only time you have it all game." Said the man. The guy that decided to guard Wyatt was imitating to say the least. He may have only been the same height as Wyatt but even under his long sleeve you could tell he was carrying some muscle.

Wyatt stuck to his guns, however, and the second they checked the ball, he chucked up a fast 3 point shot at the top of the key. A cheap move that would often annoy Rick in their pickup games.

It was a move Wyatt had gotten quite good at. Just as it had done many times before, the ball whizzed though the basket giving Wyatts team the first point of the game.

"Cocky and cheap, I guess." Said Wyatts opponent. "Whatever, man. It won't work twice."

Wyatt had wanted to hit another one and prove him wrong. However, this time when he checked the ball, his opponent was stuck on him like gum on the bottom of a shoe. There was no chance of a shot. He was just barely able to pass the ball over to Matt.

Well, in Matt's direction at least. The pass gets intercepted by the blonde guy, who spoke earlier. AJ tries to stand in his way on his trip to the basket, but the guy puts his shoulder down and bumps AJ away from him with ease, before popping up a floater that falls right through the basket.

The game was now all tied up. The opposing team had the ball. They also seemed to have found their target, because as soon as the play started, they passed to the guy being covered by AJ. He once again pushed his way through and made yet another shot.

Things were not looking good. The boys were down, and the other team just needed one point to win. Wyatt's trash talk was on the verge of being exposed for being all talk, and AJ was discovered as being the weak link in their defense.

Play starts. Again, they go back to attacking AJ. Wyatt braced himself for another made shot that would end the game. "AJ, HOLD YOUR GROUND!" Matt yells at the freshman.

AJ's pride must have kicked in. He plants his feet and puffs up his chest. He makes himself a wall that refuses to be moved by his opponent. His opponent tries to break through, but to no avail. He tries to pass it to a teammate, but AJ is there for that too.

AJ reaches out his hand at the perfect time, stealing the ball. With no one in between him and the hoop, AJ takes full advantage and puts up a layup to tie the game.

"ATTA BOY, AJ!" Wyatt calls out. The boys get back in position for another play. All the while they are celebrating their newfound favorable position of 1 point away from victory with the ball in hand. However, the game wasn't over yet, and the boys knew it. They had to give it their all to keep this opportunity from slipping through their fingers.

The ball gets checked to Wyatt but once again, he gets locked down. He manages to get a low bounce pass over to AJ, who grabs it and makes a brake for the basket. With a defender on him, it looks to everyone that he is going to try for the contested layup.

However, AJ shocks everyone on the court... everyone but Matt, that is. The two are in sync. When AJ goes for what looks to be an under-hand layup, his defender jumps to block. However, AJ throws up a lob just far enough away from the basket to pass the block. Matt jumps up and grabs the floater before slamming it down through the hoop in one swift motion.

Wyatt throws his arms up in celebration! The boys won. The court was now theirs. "Dang it!" one of the guys on the other team pouts in frustration. "Rules are rules, man... that court's yours."

Matt and AJ high five, happy to be rid of their short-lived rivalry. However, Wyatt decided that he enjoyed their game. 'Afterall' he thought 'we could all use a bit of healthy competition'.

"You fellas don't gotta run away so soon." Wyatt called out. "How about we run it back?"

The opposing team looked at each other, unsure for a moment. Soon enough, they agreed. The second game was on. The whole group battled it out, sharing the court the rest of the afternoon.

CHAPTER 13

2nd Game

   I sit on the back of the bus on route to our away game. The team doesn't take up all the seats on the bus, so I am able to sit alone. This gives me the chance to put my headphones on, and lock into the right mindset before the game.

   It's not the nicest ride in the world. The bus has multiple windows that don't close all the way, leaving about a half inch gap letting chilly outside air seep in. On top of that, it only has one heating vent located under one of the seats near the middle of the bus.

   A seat that was unsurprisingly taken by the team's seniors, John and Matt. Our freshman small forward, AJ, is in the seat behind them. Wyatt sits in the seat in front of me, also listening to his music.

   The bus is quiet, other than Coach Morgan making casual conversation with the bus driver in the first row. Our whole team has our game faces on. It's clear now that the time has come to play again, and the chance to leave tonight 0-2 is a big possibility. Everyone wants to try their best to make sure we walk out of here with a win.

   I just hope that they didn't wait too long to adjust their attitudes. However, getting a win tonight won't be easy. Our opponents on what is this cold Friday afternoon are the Mt. Billings

Billy Goats; a school over 2 hours away from our own. Last year they won 7 of their 10 games. Local sports writers say they're all set to be even better this year. To top that off, they are coming off a big win in their first game.

Because of the long drive, Coach has informed us that we'll be arriving almost as the game is scheduled to start. We'll be forced to take the court without warming up.

I stick my hands in the pockets of my brown team hoodie and hang my head looking down at my matching brown sweatpants. I try to stop my anxiety from climbing the 'what ifs' of all the possible outcomes of tonight's game play in my head.

Over all the noise of my racing mind… I can't help but hear the words of Mr. Hugh's story from Wednesday night. 'Faith in the face of fear.'

I could use a little sip of whatever Daniel was drinking when he was thrown into the lion's den. If he could handle that, I should be able to handle missing a shot in front of a crowd of people. It sounds nice; some magic being that can pick me up and save me from my own metaphorical lion's den, carrying me to a perfect ending to my story.

That's all it is, though… it's just a story. Still, it's a story that people like Shelby seem to believe. Shelby… She made good on her end of our deal and stayed after practice to help me work on my shot yesterday.

Truth be told, it frustrated me more than anything. There were more than a few critiques from Shelby, and more than a few missed shots from me. Well, I've got to believe it's going to help me in the long run.

After what feels like ages, the bus finally pulls up to the school. Coach gets out first and signals for us to follow. The school has a long concrete walkway leading up to its double door entry.

Realistically it was only about a 30-foot walk in 38-degree weather, but with the cold wind blowing through my clothes, it felt like a mile hike in the arctic.

Finally, we make it to the door. Coach holds it open for the team, and we make our way through the lunchroom. They must have served something like tacos for lunch by the smell of it. We weave through all of the lunch tables in our path until we get to a large door on the other side labeled 'Gymnasium.'

After walking through, we see that the other team is already on the court. We approach a line of chairs on the side of the court and start to strip our warmup sweats off. "All rise for the national anthem." is announced over a speaker.

We do as instructed. However, I'll admit, I don't keep my eyes glued to the flag the whole time. Instead, I use the moment to take a scan of the crowd, a crowd that is filled with the blue and yellow colors of the home team, unsurprisingly.

I search the crowd to see if there are any faces I recognize, faces like my mothers, who I am able to spot in the crowd sitting by herself. A passing thought hits me as I wonder if in times like this, she misses my dad a little more than normal. Wishing he was here to sit with her.

I decide not to dwell on the thought and instead let it pass, telling myself it will only negatively affect my play. I also can't help but notice the team must have beat Ava and Shelby here, as I don't spot them anywhere in the stands.

I am forced to refocus as the anthem ends and Coach Morgan calls for the starters to line up on the court.

John takes the center of the court, ready to go for the jump ball. Wyatt and I take our spots behind him. AJ and Matt line up on each side of John. The referee walks out with the game ball and my heart starts to beat a little harder with every step he takes.

I had some nerves before every jump in track, but those nerves were routine. They were something I had gotten used to from years and years of preparation. Yet despite pouring my life into basketball for the last months of my life, these nerves still feel different in some way. Basketball took me so quickly by storm, I guess I never truly had time to acclimate.

I'm given no time to calm my nerves as before I know it the ball is in the air and the whistle is blown. Both John and the opposing teams center make a jump for it. The other center is a big man in his own right, but still not as stocky as John. No surprise there. However, he may have an inch on John in the height department.

That inch may have been the difference maker because the Billy Goats win the tip off. We now have the job of defending. We each quickly find our men and chase them down. The other team's point guard, who I have the pleasure of guarding tonight, wears number 1 on his jersey.

He happens to be taller and broader than me. which is once again no surprise… unfortunately. It looks like I'll have my work cut out for me.

The first quarter turns out to be a hard-fought 8 minutes with little scoring happening from either side. By the end of it, all players on the court are beathing hard from how many trips we've taken up and down the court.

The score sits tight but we're trailing. Billy Goats-14, Stags-12. Wyatt, Matt, and AJ have all scored, with Wyatt being responsible for 6 of our points. John and I have yet to get our first buckets.

Every time John has had the ball in the paint, the kid guarding me pulls off to double team John. This leaves me open at the 3-point line, but John just keeps trying to force it in instead of passing back to me.

"John, if you're getting double teamed, that means someone else is open! In this case, it's Rick! Pass it back to him so we can steal some 3-pointers!" Coach Morgan explains to John on the sideline before we go out to play the 2nd quarter.

"Coach, I have a better shot of hitting a shot in double coverage than Rick does of hitting a 3." John says.

Coach puts his hand over his face and shakes his head. He looks to me like he's hoping for me to argue my case. I stay silent.

"Look, it's happened three times now. If Rick just made one of those, we would be winning now, right?!" Coach tells John.

"...Right"

"Then just do what I'm telling you! Now get back out there, it's go time."

The team runs back onto the court. I started to as well, but I am stopped by a hand grabbing my bicep. Coach Morgan stops me just before I get back on the court. He smiles at me, making each end of his mustache rise. "You've got this, Rick." He says, before slapping me on the back and sending me on my way.

We start the quarter with the ball. As is standard, John passes in the ball to me. As I begin down the court, the defense comes up to guard. They're not going make it easy on me it seems, must not want me getting any fast break chances.

I'm forced to make some good moves to get down court, but I manage to do so. However, once I approach the 3-point line, the coverage lets up. The guy guarding me splits the difference between me at the 3 line and John under the basket. Just as they have been all game, they're ready to double cover John.

It looks like the time to test my shooting is here. 'You've got this, Rick.' The words of Coach run though my head. 'God... if you really are a thing, do you mind giving me a little bit of the magic you gave to Daniel?' I think to myself, mostly joking, but with a little grain of hope that it will somehow actually help me sink this shot.

I fake the pass to John and the defense bites hard, leaving me even more wide open than I already was. I jump up and release my shot. It takes a high arching path towards the basket before coming through the net making one of the best sounds I have ever heard. 'swoosh'

The home crowd doesn't make a sound, but the few Stag fans in the building go nuts! Most of all, my mom.

I see Coach Morgan clapping as well as we switch to defense. Before I know it, we're back in the same situation on offense again. This time John has the ball. Once again, my guard pulls off me to double team John.

Unlike the first quarter, however, John loops the ball behind his head, passing to me. For the second time in a row, I hit the open 3-point shot, a feat I once thought I would never be able to pull off.

We had the Goats all figured out from that point on. Any time the defense tried to guard me, I passed to John, who could hit the layup in single coverage. If they tried to stop him, I hit the open 3.

We had them in shambles and we won the game 59- 44. A game in which I had 18 points made off all 3-point shots. I also got 10 assists on John's 20 points in the paint.

More than any of that, I proved I deserve to be a starter on this team. I proved this is a lineup that can win games, and against good opponents at that.

As our team cheered and smiled on our way out of the Mount Billings High School, I feel unbeatable. I can't even imagine 2-0 feeling nearly as good as 1-1 feels in this moment.

Without the pain of the loss, the work it took to EARN this win may have never taken place. The win itself didn't magically make everything better. However, the skill and newfound confidence it took to get the win makes me sure that there are more wins on the horizon.

CHAPTER 14

After Party

The whole team was over the moon. On the bus ride back, even guys that don't normally talk were acting like the best of chums. Nothing could bring us down from the high we were riding from our win.

Even Coach Morgan got in on the comradery, sitting back and laughing with us kids instead of his normal spot up front with the driver. About an hour into our drive, he said "Hey driver, stop right up here." referring to a large restaurant with a neon green lit sign reading 'PZZA SLICEZ'. The 'I' must had gone out.

"I would say these kids have earned a few victory slices, on me." He said. It reminded me of when my dad would offer to take me for victory chocolate shakes after every track meet.

It's weird though. For the first time since I lost him... the memory of him doesn't hurt. Sure, I miss him like crazy, but tonight, instead of letting it bum me out... I just take the good memory for what it is... good, and heartwarming. I let it add to the joy that I am already feeling as we pull into the parking lot and load off the bus.

Once inside, the place is empty, other than a few locals getting a late dinner. Coach Morgan paid at the counter and the team was unleashed to go through a buffet line of different pizzas sitting comfy under warming lights.

Pepperoni, sausage, supreme, BBQ chicken, and many more, all with hot melted cheese on top. In other words, it was paradise for a group of hungry teenage athletes.

I fix my plate behind Wyatt, who loads his plate up with more pizza than I suspect his skinny frame can hold. After we plate our mountains of pizza, we walk back to a table big enough to seat the whole team.

Wyatt doesn't even wait to sit down as I see him snacking on a slice on the walk over to the table. "BRO!" he exclaims as we take our seats. "I think I died and went to heaven." Wyatt jokes, stuffing his face.

I chuckle before taking a few bites of my own. We don't get too far into our meal before the savory food dries our mouths and we realize we forgot to get drinks. "Hang tight, man. I'll run up and grab us some sodas." I tell Wyatt.

"Brotha, you really are the team MVP tonight." he jokingly thanks me.

I slowly jog to the other side of the restaurant, out of view to of the rest of the team, to where they have the soda machine. In a hurry to get back to my meal, I fill up two cups quickly.

In all my rush, I don't even look up before turning to head back to the table. Unfortunately, I didn't notice a guy standing behind me in line. I turn into him, dumping 2 ice cold sodas all over the front of his clothes.

"HEY" the guy yells. "What's the matter with you!" He's a middle-aged man, about my size. He was wearing a classic Iowa get up. Jeans, boots, and a Hawkeye's hoodie. He topped it all off with a bald head and an angry looking face surrounded by stubble.

"Oh man. I am so sorry. I wasn't paying attention at all." I try to explain. "You're darn right you weren't paying attention! What are you, stupid?!" he starts his ticked off rant at me.

"Just chill out, sir. I'll go ask if they have any towels so we can dry you off."

"Chill out?! You ruin my dinner out and I'm the one that needs to chill out?! You dumb kid! Someone needs to teach you how to treat an adult!" his voice starts to raise louder. The distance between us starts to shrink and his chest puffs out.

I try to deescalate the situation, but I keep my eyes locked on the man as my concern grows that he may get violent. I am so focused on him in fact, that I didn't notice the hulking figure creeping up behind him.

A large hand drops on the man's shoulder as a stern voice calmly says "Have we got a problem over here?". The man turns to look fear in the eye as John Lynn stands towering over him.

The man is forced to take a step back. He would've nearly fallen into me if I hadn't moved out of the way. "Yeah... this uh... this kid here got my clothes soaked." The man says, clearly a bit nervous now.

"Here's what's going to happen now," John starts. "My friend and I are going to go back to our table. You're going to find a towel or use napkins, for all I care. Problem solved." John states and gives me a look like 'come on.'

I start to follow him back to our table before the man says "Well," John quickly whips his head around and glares at him, seeming ready to throw down. "...yeah, alright." is all that comes out of the guy's mouth.

John and I have the opportunity for a brief conversation as we walk back to our seats. "That was intense, man. I mean, I did accidently spill my drink on that guy." I say.

"You could have done it on purpose for all I care." John answers "I didn't like the way that guy was talking to you. You're my teammate... I got your back."

As we get back to the table, I find myself feeling grateful for one of the first times that John is my teammate. I take my seat next to Wyatt who blankly stares at me. "What?" I ask.

He throws his arms up "Bro! Where's our drinks?"

CHAPTER 15

Winter Break

"Welcome to Trinity Ranch!" Mr. Hugh shouts, holding his arms out in a 'ta da' pose. The land was filled with open range and livestock. Horses of all sorts run in a large pin behind Mr. Hugh, while about fifty yards to the right sit two medium-sized wood cabins. Each cabin has a large wood carved sign over them reading 'COWBOYS' or 'COWGIRLS'.

It was official... we had arrived at church camp. Shelby had changed up our deal and decided it was mandatory that I come in order to continue our shooting lessons. Needless to say, I was forced to come. In turn, I forced my friends Wyatt and Ava to come so I wouldn't have any awkward moments by myself out here.

I'll admit, however, I am looking forward to the break, even if it is somewhere out of my element. The team has been playing our hearts out. We've had 2 more games since playing the Billy Goats. We won both, making us a solid 3-1. Couple that with me getting double doubles in all 3 of our wins, I'd say I've earned a break.

Everyone collects over by Mr. Hugh. "Here we're going do some fun ranch activities such as roping and horseback riding. Then, later in the day, we'll do a lesson before getting some smores ready by the campfire." Mr. Hugh gives the itinerary. "All I need to know now, is... who wants to ride first?"

Wyatt's hand shoots up almost fast enough to leave his coat sleeve behind. "Alright! Come up here and we'll get you saddled up!" Mr. Hugh says.

"You better not hurt yourself." Ava warns Wyatt before he heads up.

"Unfortunately, I can make no promises." Wyatt answers her before heading up to the front, leaving both Ava and I behind. Ava staying back with me makes me very happy that I brought 2 friends instead of just the 1.

Wyatt walks up to Mr. Hugh, who puts his hand on Wyatt's shoulder. "Alright, a newcomer! What's your name, son?"

"Wyatt Herbert."

"Well, I am sure you'll be a regular John Wayne, Herbert. Let's get you saddled up."

The crowd's attention turns to the action going on in the front. This includes the attention of Shelby Cunningham, who I spot near the front of said crowd. She must have gotten here a little before us. Her naturally curly hair sticks out from her sock hat. She's wearing jeans and a bomber jacket, which catches me eye as I'm used to only seeing her in sweats with her hair up.

Around that time, Ava's attention turns to me. She must have seen me looking over at Shelby. "So, what's the gameplan here, Rick? Do you need me to walk you over there so you can start a conversation with her?" Ava asks with a sly attitude.

"If only it was that simple." I respond before realizing how eager that makes me sound to go talk to her. "Err, I mean... I don't know what you're talking about."

"Oh please! Someone as blind as Saul on the road to Damascus could tell you like her."

I raise my eyebrow to that response, truly having no clue what she was talking about. "What? I'm taking world religion.

I thought I'd keep my witty banter on theme for this church event you decided we need to accompany you on." She claims.

I can't say I'm surprised that Ava already knows more than me on this Christian stuff. She is an A+ student, after all. She knows more than me about... well pretty much everything.

She does have a point. Maybe I feel too weird saying it out loud, but I do like spending time with Shelby. Staying late after practice with her is the most fun part of my day.

I also can't help but admire her attitude towards life. With every passing Wednesday that she brings me to church, I think I understand a little more about what makes her the way she is.

Alright. Yeah. I can go talk to her. I do it after practice every day. Ugh, but that's so different than here. We have something to talk about there. If I really want to get closer to her we can't just have all of our talks be about basketball. How do I even go about starting random small talk with her. Alright, I can feel myself over thinking this. I just need to walk up to her and say 'Hello'.

As I wait for my bravery to kick in, I hear a truck kicking up dirt behind us. I turn to see John peeling in at high speeds. Both him and Matt climb out of the truck, and head straight to Shelby. "Sorry we're late." He says as they approach.

I feel like John and I's friendship took a good step forward the other night. However, I don't yet feel comfortable trying to flirt in front of him. So, unfortunately, I hold back, deciding that now just isn't the right time. I instead hang back with Ava as we watch Wyatt parade around on his horse. I'm all the while hoping that this trip will bring another opportunity.

CHAPTER 16

Most Valuable Lesson

Most of the kids ended up riding horses. There were other activities for us to try, however, we all lined up to take turns trying to rope a fake bull. We also got to hand feed grain to some real ones.

Soon enough, it was time for the main reason of the trip; to learn more about God. Just as the sun was heading down, we started a very sizable campfire. With a little help from propane heaters that were scattered around, it did the job of keeping all of us warm.

Mr. Hugh started his lesson as the sky went from a quite nice pink color to a shade of black. "Alright, I know we're all hyped up to get hot dogs and smores going." He began. "So, I am going to speak briefly, but I am also going to speak from the heart." In my short time knowing Mr. Hugh I already know that if he is speaking from that heart, one thing is for sure, it's not going to be brief. At that my stomach starts to growl, almost like it's yelling at me for waiting so long to feed it. despite the rest of my body being genuinely interested in what Mr. Hugh has to say.

His normally bubbly personality got a bit flatter. "How many of you have ever messed up in your life?" he asked. The hands of some of the more extroverted kids raised. While the rest of us introverts stayed still. Although I felt the urge to raise mine, I didn't follow through. He keeps on "If you didn't raise your hand, don't worry. You're young, you've still got plenty of time." he joked, which got a few halfhearted laughs.

"If you did raise your hand, then I am right there with you. You see; to be honest, I have messed up more times than I could ever hope to remember. And there's more than one time that I do remember, that still haunts me to this day. There was a time in my life when I wouldn't even come near a church. A big reason being was I knew in my head that I wasn't worth being saved anyway.

Little did I know at the time, nobody has earned their way into being saved. When someone finally cared enough to give me a Bible, and when I had finally hit a low enough point to where I thought it couldn't hurt to read it, my life view got flipped on its head.

When I read the words of a man, that had been beaten, that had been hurt, that had spilled his own blood, all the while being innocent, the only sinless man to ever walk... when I read Luke 23:34 'then Jesus said, father forgive them, for they know not what they do.' I realized the power that the love of God holds on this world. He died to FORGIVE us of our sins, making our sins today part of the reason he had to be nailed to that cross.

So, when He forgave that day, he didn't only forgive the men that whipped him and put that crown of thorns on him. He forgave us for all the dumb mistakes we make in today's world, also. The only thing He asks in return is for us to love him back, as well as try and extend the same love and kindness He showed us back to our fellow man.

I just wanted to remind all of you that today. I love you all, but more importantly, Jesus loves you!... Alright, now we can cook some smores." Mr. Hugh finishes his lengthy story with a chuckle.

While not the longest lesson of his I've listened to, I believe it hit home more than any of them so far. One look at Wyatt and Ava and I can tell it had them think hard about the love of God as well. Some kids near the front seemed to be brought to tears, though it could have just been the cold air making their noses run.

One thing was clear to me, however; that being if God himself could forgive people that treated him so poorly, I had a responsibility to try and do the same. And there was one person that came to mind instantly that I needed to extend that forgiveness to...

CHAPTER 17

What We Find in the Flames

Ashes cracking off of smoldering wood fills the night air. The sun makes its retreat around the edge of our sight as we feast on hot dogs and marshmallows. Soon, the flames become our only source of light.

Bales of hay work nicely as seats for us all around the fire, if not a little pokey. I must say I have a great time hanging out with Wyatt and Ava, joking around in this new environment. Still, something is pulling my attention away from just enjoying their company.

Or rather someone. I catch myself having to purposely not look in Shelbys direction or else my body will do it instinctively. I never really put any focus on girls before in my life. My dad and I were always so eaten up with sports... I guess I felt I never had any extra effort I wanted to put towards a crush. Crush?... Yeah, I guess it's fair to say that's what this is at this point.

Yeah, I thought she was cute from the start. I also think she's a great time hanging out with. I never wanted a crush to develop though... unfortunately I guess that's all it takes. You can't always prepare for this sort of thing. It just happens.

As the night goes on, some of the other kids start to turn in. Wyatt and Ava get tired too and their energy starts to wither away. As Ava rests her head on Wyatt's shoulder, I start to feel like even more of a 3rd wheel than normal.

"Well, that's my sign to get off to bed." I joke. I bid them a goodnight before starting my unenthused walk to the cabin I am not looking forward to sharing with a dozen other dudes.

Before I get too far, I hear "Hey Joseph, I got a seat for ya." from Shelby, calling me over. Patting an empty spot on the bail of hay beside her, singling for me to take a seat. She must have moved seats when she saw me get up. I move over to sit next to her. "Hey! I was wondering if we would get a chance to talk, seeing as you're the one who dragged me out here." I joke with her.

"Oh please." She laughs. "You know coming out here has been worth it."

"You're right. I admit, Mr. Hugh has a way with words... really makes you think."

"Yeah. Trying to unlock the meaning of life can do that to a person." She tells me, never losing her playful attitude.

I take a pause, looking at her charming smile towards me. "Honestly, I owe you a thanks." I say. "These last few months, helping me with basketball and dragging me to church... it's meant a lot to me. I was in a little bit of a low place there for a second."

I'm typically a man of few words. The ones I choose to say aren't normally about my feelings, so I am not so good at sharing them. Shelby starts to respond. "Hey, don't thank me too much. I am just living vicariously through your basketball career since I can't play right now... and I suppose hanging out with you doesn't completely suck." She states, rolling her eyes with a sarcastic grin.

I let out a laugh that we share together before yet again the only sound being the cracking of the fire and light conversions of the other kids nearby.

I can't let the pause in the conversation stay too long. This is probably the best chance I have to ask her to hangout in a non-basketball related setting. For some reason, I feel the same nerves I do before the start of a game. As I've been learning recently though, I can't let my anxieties stop me from taking my shot.

"Well, then maybe we could hangout more when we get back? ... You know, as long as it doesn't COMPLETELY suck." I say with my best confident impression to make it as clear as I can that I am asking for a date.

Her smile widens. "Yeah! Sounds like fun." She says in a soft voice.

I smile while looking at the fire. I am happy my offer was actually accepted. As the night hours take their toll, the few kids left by the fire become quiet. After a while of siting in silence, I am surprised to feel Shelby's head rest on my shoulder.

I play it cool and don't move, worried that any reaction might make her move. We enjoy the next hour or so together making conversation and learning more about each other. Things we didn't know we had in common, and ways we are both different and unique. Soon the night wears on and it's time to say goodnight before heading our separate ways and off to bed.

CHAPTER 18

Christmas

An old Christmas movie was the only thing serving to kill the awkwardness between my mother and I as Christmas morning was finally here. A day I always look forward to... but now, like so many other things, feels a little off without my dad.

Sure, it's been over half a year now. I do feel like I've come a long way mentally, but looking at only two stockings hung up this year still feels wrong. One is labeled 'R' for myself and the other 'V' for my mom Violet.

Not having my dad help me get gifts for my mom this year like we normally did early every December will most likely leave her disappointed in what she ends up with. He had a way of getting her to admit what she wanted. The trick is you can't just outright ask her, he'd say. Unless you want a "You don't have to get me anything." response.

You have to make it come up naturally so she doesn't get what you're asking her. Say things like "I saw this today, wouldn't it be fun to have one of those?" and then gage her reaction. Dad always said I'd need to use that trick on my future wife and that women took a lot of perception to figure out what they're thinking sometimes.

I didn't do any of that this year. Mix my lack of 'perception' along with me not having a job, and my mom ended up with socks this year.

I got some new athletic shorts and a sock hat in return. Conversation between me and my mom has been good lately. It wasn't easy, but over time we've learned to navigate the ins and outs of being by ourselves in this house. Its strange, right of the bat losing my Dad seemed to push us apart, as we both needed to heal in our own ways. As time goes on however little by little we have learned to lean on one another. In fact a dare say we are down a road to becoming closer then ever, and a different kind of friendship then we had before is starting to form.

We've learned what stories to tell that bring smiles to each other, and what stories to avoid if we don't want to end up in tears. However, on a day with as many memories as Christmas day, the water gets a little hard to sail through. Dad is clearly on both of our minds. One wrong step and our talks today could crack an eggshell, making an opening for tears running down our hardwood floors.

We're both sitting side by side on our brown couch in our PJ's. Mom is drinking her coffee while I decided to go with hot chocolate as it seemed more festive. I also didn't feel like the added anxiety of caffeine would do me any favors.

"Your dad aways liked this movie." My mom states. I knew she wouldn't be able to help herself. A part of me just wanted to make it through today. Still, I can't blame her. If there is one thing that today is missing, it's my father. Talking about him, even if it's hard to do, still makes him a part of this day with us.

"Yeah... He did." I say back.

"Do you remember how he would always give you a hard time for not putting out milk and cookies for Santa? Even after you became a teenager." She laughed.

"Well, he just wanted a good excuse to cheat on his diet." I joke back with her.

"That reminds me, I have one more thing I want you to have today." She says as she gets up and walks to her room. I sit there waiting in anticipation.

On her way back, the floor creaks as she steps off the soft carpet of her bedroom and back on to the hard wood.

"I know you just got back from your big church trip, so I thought now would be the perfect time to give you this." She says pulling a newer looking Bible out from behind her back.

"Uh... Thank you, mom... but the church already gave me one." I tell her, hoping not to seem ungrateful.

"I know... but this one belonged to your father."

My eyes focused in on the brown book after hearing that. "Dad had a Bible? He never said anything... the only time I ever heard him say 'God' was after 'oh my' or before 'dang it.'

"Well, that was true until about 4 months before his accident. He came home one day and told me someone finally explained God to him in a way that made him think. He said he was excited to learn more, and we went out and purchased this that night."'

"Why didn't he say anything to me?"

"He was trying to read the whole thing first. He took explaining it to us very seriously and didn't want to say anything wrong. He was even researching churches we could try."

I haven't given a ton of thought about where my dad is in the afterlife yet, being a new believer myself. When I learned about hell a part of me never wanted to think of the chance that he could be there. However, this news changes all of that. This gives me real hope that my dad is up above me.

"Did he ever say that he for sure believed it?" I ask

"Oh yes! In his last months he said it all the time. He would say 'Jesus is Lord' almost every night. That's all he would tell me though, other than him being happy that he was getting close to being comfortable explaining it to us."

She hands me the book as I smile up at her. "When he passed, I thought about trying to read it, but I never did. A part of me thought I would never hear about it again until your little friend invited you to church... God must be pretty determined to make His way into this home, I suppose." She smiles.

I start to flip through the book catching glimpses of highlighter marks on the pages of verses he must have liked. One verse in particular catches my eye and I stop to read. It was near his bookmark so it must have been as far as he got before he died.

Romans 10:9 "If you openly declare that Jesus is Lord and believe in your heart that God raised him from the dead, you will be saved."

My heart gets warm and I realize how great of a Christmas this is shaping up to be. Because even though I was prepared for it to be the worst one without my dad being here. I see now that this house is just as full as it ever has been. God may have been waiting at the door for a while now, but this year we finally let him in.

CHAPTER 19

Letting Go

The next day there was something on my mind that I needed to get done. I got the address I needed. Thankfully, it was only a few miles away. I thought doing this in front of my mom would make things hard, so I embarked on my cold walk alone. Rather than having her drive me.

Bundled up from head to toe, I think of what I'm going to say when I get there. I begin boggling my mind on every small detail, including how many times I should knock on the door. I run through all the things to say as I truck through the falling snow hitting me in the face in winter so thick that I can hardly see the sidewalk.

When the house I am aiming for is finally in sight, I breathe a sigh of relief from my hurting lungs. Taking a hike through the snow has proved to be just as hard as Coach Morgan punishing us with extra cardio. I step up the wooden porch steps, hoping the words will come to me when the door is answered. Man, I am out of breath.

I raise my tired arm and pound on the door 4 times. I try and catch my breath while waiting. Unfortunately, I don't have the time to as the door swings open all but immediately. "...Rick? Is that you."

huff "Hello Ms. Jenifer." *huff* "Sorry to" *huff* "drop in unannounced." I say, as she looks up at me in confusion. Sounds of a crying toddler can be heard coming from inside the house. Ms. Jenifer was definitely taken by surprise with my visit. Seeing her dressed in sweats with her short blonde hair in a wreck makes me feel like I've interrupted a lazy day. That's not what she says, however. "No need to be sorry. Come inside out of the cold."

From the day this woman has entered my life, I have resented her, even though she's been nothing but kind to my mom and I. None of that mattered to me because she was involved in my dad's accident. She lived when he passed away. Nothing she could have done would ever make me feel like I didn't get the short end of the stick.

However, none of that was her fault. It wasn't anyone's fault. Sometimes life hits you like a truck and responding with bitterness and hate... just makes the world grey around you. In truth, I could have spent the rest of my life blaming this woman standing in front of me, but it would only stand to hurt us both. Forgiveness has its place in the story of how I handle my dad's passing, and I am putting it to practice right here and now.

"That's okay ma'am, I just came over here to say one thing to you." As the words come out of my mouth, I can see her emotions brace for impact. Afterall, I've been short with her in every conversation we've had. She probably thinks I'm here to yell at her.

"And that is... that it wasn't your fault." I don't even know if she feel's like it was, so hopefully she doesn't take me saying that the wrong way. Still in my weaker moments I play the blame game on her. I don't think she would have tried to become close to my mom and I if she didn't carry any guilt over the accident. Even if she wasn't at any fault at all in reality, This is something I need to say to her.

Her eyes immediately begin to swell, and her shoulders relax, like pent up emotion is being released in her just by me saying that one sentence. I keep at it. "I am truly sorry if my cold actions made you feel like I blame you, but I don't anymore. I have chosen to let go of all of that. You and your child... my dad did the right thing by saving you. I couldn't be prouder of him for that."

At this point tears are rolling down her face as she grabs me up in a hug. Both of her arms around both of mine, the tears on her cheek wetting the shoulder of my winter jacket. We hold our hug for a moment before she wipes her tears and breaks the silence. "Thank you, Rick. Are you sure you don't want to come in and warm up? I can make you some hot coffee?"

"No, I will be just fine... I still have one more person to talk to today." I say with a smile.

"Okay. If there's ever anything I can do for you, please let me know."

"Thank you... I appreciate that."

I hear her door shut behind me as I turn and walk away. Although, I don't make it very far before sitting down on one of her snow-covered porch steps. I take a brief moment before looking up and begin to come up with the words to describe my feelings. "Hey dad, its me." I make the choice not to care if I look like an odd ball talking in the snow alone.

"I owe you an apology as well. All you ever did was fight to give me a good life. Well, this year... it wasn't so good. I was so mad at you all summer. For not being there. Not helping me train for track. Not being there to sit with me and mom to eat dinner. Shoot, one night mom tried to make your casserole that I always like so much... it didn't taste the same. I was REALLY mad at you that night.

I see it differently now. I see you were just doing what you thought was right. As I told Ms. Jenifer before, I could not be prouder of you dad. I forgive you. I can't wait to see you again.

I love you." With those words, I stand up and start my walk home.

CHAPTER 20

Playoff's

Yeah, life was good! Winter break ended and basketball was back in full swing. January games came and went, and we kept our win streak alive. Sure, they weren't all blow outs, but it still felt like we were unbeatable. With every game, we grew as a team. I barely had to think if I should pass it to Wyatt for the 3, or if I should bounce pass inside to Matt for the driving mid-range jumper. We were all in sync! I even had a few highlight reel dunks that will be great to send to colleges, videos courtesy of my mom's phone. I'll just need to mute her cheering before I send them, don't want the recruiters to go deaf.

Most importantly, we were 11-1 going into the playoffs, giving us the home court advantage in our first game. Although we didn't get exactly the match up we wanted, our opponents are the Huxley Hurricanes. We have a better record, seeing as they are 9-3. However, a lot of people think they are a sleeper team to win the whole state championship. All that hype is mostly due to their senior point guard. 6'5, D1 commit to Missouri, Aidan Green.

This is the man I will have the pleasure of trying to guard in just a few short hours. This all brings me to now. My team and I are listening to some hype up music in the locker room, trying to convince ourselves further that we will become state champions this year. "Yep, that'll do it." AJ says plainly, causing the rest of us to look over his way. "What?" Matt asks.

"The way this song is hitting right now, I think I may just drop 30 tonight." He's referring to the rather aggressive rap song he has blaring. Some of the guy's chuckle at him, seeing as he hasn't come close to hitting 30 points all season.

"Hey, I am all for it. Whatever gets us out of here with a win." Says Wyatt as he stretches near his locker. "Ah, you don't gotta be worried about winning at all. I've lead you guys this far, haven't I?" AJ rebuttals.

"YOU'VE lead us?" John raises his eyebrow as he sits slumped against his own locker. "But of course." AJ proudly states while pointing his thumb toward his chest.

"Pffh. Whatever you say, man." John replies with a chuckle, keeping with the lighthearted tone of the conversion.

"GENTELMEN!" The echoing voice of Coach Morgan enters the locker room along with the rest of him. All of us kids turn our undivided attention to Coach as if he is our drill sergeant.

He looks to us; his starting five. We're the ones he needs playing at our very best if we are going to go on and win this game. "Listen boys, it's been quite the season. I mean 11 wins in a row?!" The whole team claps, cheering on our accomplishment. "We haven't lost since our first game. You know what that is? Improvement. Week in and week out we get BETTER! Old Coach Morgan can't ask for more than that. John and Matt, you boys are our seniors... you have stepped up and become the leaders I hoped you would be this year." Matt and John both give a look of thanks to Coach for his words.

"AJ, at the start of the year, you couldn't stop a paper bag from getting to the basket. But now? Shoot, you can play defense with the best of your teammates. Wyatt, when I first named you a starter, I wasn't sure if your lazy attitude would ever allow you to care about winning a basketball game. But every time I watch you play now, I know you're fighting to get the win with all you got in you, son. Rick, at the start of this season, all I knew about you was that I had never seen a little guy jump like you do. Over the course of this season, however, I have watched you go from being just an athlete... to a true, complete basketball player. All you boys have earned the right to be here. Go out there and show how much you've grown tonight."

"YEAH!!!" We all cheer at the conclusion of the motivating speech.

From there, it's time to head over to the tunnel. The crowd above our heads are already plenty loud. From the sounds of it, it's a packed house tonight. "LADYS AND GENETLEMEN! ITS TIME FOR THE STAGS TO MAKE THEIR WAY TO THE COURT!!!" The crowd erupts into cheering as the announcer begins to introduce us. "FIRST UP, YOUR STAGS CENTER, NUMER 91; JOHN LYNN!"

John nods at us before running out to the center of the court as the crowd cheers him on. One by one my team gets called out. "Hey." Wyatt looks over to me "We're going leave it all out there tonight... win or lose." He says, holding his fist out to me.

"...Yeah." I say, bumping his fist with mine. His name gets called and he makes his entrance. It's odd seeing him so serious. I guess we have grown a lot this year. "NOW YOUR STAGS POINT GUARD! NUMBER 36; RICK JOSEPH!"

I make my jog out there. It's so loud it's hard to think. The first thing I notice is Shelby and Ava sitting together. Not too far behind them, I see my mom and Ms. Jenifer. I am happy they all made it. This game won't be easy so I'll need the support. The next thing I lock my eyes on is the other team. The Huxley Hurricanes.

They're wearing solid black jerseys with silver print. Most of them are wearing black shoes to match. By the looks of it, size wise, we actually match up pretty well against them. Other than one stand out. One outlier; the match up at point guard. Aidan Green vs myself.

I bring my gaze to him. I can already tell this won't be easy. He's tall, and carrying an athletic build fit for a D1 athlete. His black curly hair ends with a low fade around his ears, revealing his studded earrings. His mere body language gives off confidence. Joking around with his teammates, not taking warmups seriously. It's as if it's a direct insult, as if he hasn't even thought about the chance that he won't be able to score on me. I grind my teeth.

If I do make it out of this town and on to a D1 team, I am going to have to face guys like this at every game. Tonight is the night I show I have what it takes. While the referee signals for us to move into position to start the game, I keep my eyes locked on Green, like I am commanding respect. I am letting him know I won't be intimidated.

My stare becomes something he takes notice of as he shrugs his abnormally long arms at me. I don't care. I don't care if it looks weird. I don't care if it doesn't make sense. This could be my last game of my junior year. I need to come with everything I have in me.

The whistle blows. The ball is thrown in the air. John jumps for it, but it evades his reach. The other team's center gets the tip. The ball flies through the air and lands in the hands of Green.

"GET ON HIM, RICK. FULL COURT PRESS! I NEED YOU TO BE THE THORN IN THAT GUY'S SIDE THIS WHOLE GAME!" Coach screams from the side.

I am already one step ahead of him though. I sprint past both John and the Huxley center and head straight for my target. As I get closer and closer I see him dribbling the ball in open space. I'll make him pay for taking me lightly by stealing that ball right from his grasp. With him in a light jog towards me, I power on full speed ahead at him and go right for the ball he is dribbling in front of him.

I lunge, reaching out with my whole body getting close enough to practically feel the rubber on my fingertips... but at the last possible moment, he pulls it away. He bounces the ball behind his back quickly into his other hand, leaving me stumbling directly past him. There is an audible "OOOO" from the crowd as I regain my footing, barley managing not to fall over in the process. I am left with a perfect view of the number 20 on Aidan Green's back as none of my teammates make it in time to stop him from slamming the ball in with a dunk and taking the lead 2-0.

John takes the ball from the referee and yells "Hey. That's alright, Rick. Shake it off." Wyatt joins in with some words as well. "Yeah, it's our turn now, show what you got, bro!"

Their words hit me about as soon as the ball goes off the pass in from John. I turn to take it down the court but am instantly met with the towering body of Aidan. Are they full court pressing us? No. I can see around him, barely. The rest of his team is on the other side of the court. It's just him pressing. Why do that? In any case, I recognize I am in trouble and look for the pass. Even with my view being blocked, I catch a glimpse of Wyatt. I try for the quick chest pass in his direction just needing to get some space from my opponent. WAIT NO! Green reaches out his long wingspan with astounding speed. He intercepts the ball midflight. "No way!" I mutter as he dribbles past me and lays in the ball for another 2 points.

I can't believe this! It's only the start of the first half and I am already being picked apart. I'm going to have to adjust, or this game is going to get out of hand. John inbounds the ball again. This time, he thinks wiser about passing in to me and throws it over to Wyatt who brings it down court. I try to break free and get open, but nothing works. Green is stuck to me like glue. Wyatt, however, manages to pass over to Matt who hits a driving layup that barely goes in. 2-4 with Huxley in the lead.

Huxley throws the ball in. I cover Green, doing my best to keep him from getting the ball. Thankfully, they pass it to their shooting guard instead. Once they bring it down, we play tight defense. Huxley isn't able to get any good looks to make a shot and their time is almost up. I use my speed to keep up with Green. If I can just keep him from getting the ball it'll be the first good thing I've done this whole game.

Sure enough, as the shot clock winds down, they look Green's way. They throw him a high lob. I reach up to steal it. The ball goes higher than my reach will allow me to go. However, it's just the right height for the long arms of Green. He snags it and jacks up a 3-point shot that falls in for him. With that made shot, I start to wonder if there is anything I can do to stop this guy.

That kind of play keeps up for the rest of the first half. I don't give in and accept my defeat. I fight tooth and nail, making every point Green scores be a point he has to to work for. Unfortunately, he still scores a lot of them. Our team, on the other hand, is all but left without a point guard on offense as no matter how hard I try to break free, I remain under the close guard of Aidan Green.

The score is 28-45 at half. I am practically fuming with frustration at my own play. To be honest, I am not sure why Coach hasn't pulled me from the game. I brace myself for cruel words from my teammates as we enter the huddle. "Bring it in, boys." Coach demands as we approach him.

"Obviously it's not going good out there right now, but that's about to change." He says with a faint smile. Here it comes, he's going to put me on the bench. "Because…" Coach keeps on as I prepare for my being pulled out of the game. "Their star player is dog tired."

His statement comes out of left field to my ears. Could he be right? How much effort could Green have really used up at this point in the game?

"He's right, Rick. Their point guard is doing all he can to keep up with you on defense. They can normally afford to make him carry the team on both sides of the ball... but it doesn't look like he's used to having to guard someone who moves as much as you do." John interjects.

"He's exactly right. His lungs have got to be on fire at this point. I can see it in his face." Coach says. "These here are championship rounds, boys. It's time to crank up the heat even hotter. John, I want you to pass it in to Rick again. Rick, if you get in trouble, bounce pass away. That, mixed with your height, should get under his arms. AJ, every time we're in the enemy's side of the court, set screens on Green. Open Rick up for a 3 and make Green work even harder to try and stop it. We're going make these kids burn out, got it?!"

The whistle blows. My team and I take the court knowing we have an uphill climb ahead if we want any chance of winning this game. I hadn't noticed before because I was too busy trying to keep up with Aidan, but I think Coach is right. He's wearing down. I can see him wiping a steady stream of sweat off his forehead, and if I pay close attention, I can see the rise and fall of his chest letting air in at a higher rate than the start of the game.

John inbounds the ball right to my hands. Sure enough, Aidan steps up to guard. I let him get close before I bounce the ball just out of reach of his wingspan. The ball makes it safely over to Wyatt who makes a run for it down the court. I take off sprinting as well, which prompts a response from Aidan. I force him to sprint right along with me, or risk leaving me open.

Once on the other side of the court, Wyatt holds the ball at the top of the key. I keep my movement high, weaving through enemy defenders in hopes of putting more obstacles in the way of Green's pursuit of me. It works like a charm. I cut right between Wyatt and the Huxley shooting guard. Aidan Green trails so closely he doesn't have time to react to his own teammate.

They crash into each other, leaving both Wyatt and I open for a second of time.

As both defenders are closer to Wyatt than me, he makes the choice to pass it my way. This allows me to hit the mid-range shot, my first points of the night. It does little to close the gap, but it's a step in the right direction. I know that if I start scoring now, there's no way they are going to pull Green out for a breather. They are going to need their best player in the game to guard me and ensure they move on to the next round of the playoffs.

With 15 points away from the lead still, I need to play some real lock down defense to keep Huxley's lead from growing. With our whole team playing full court press, the Huxley center is having a horrible time trying to find an open man. This tells me I need to be ready. Every time they get in trouble, they go to their best player, Aidan. He is currently leaving a pool of sweat in his wake as I chase him around the court. I've got to give him credit. He's clearly running on fumes, but he's still playing hard. He has the work ethic to get to the next level if I am judging him on his performance tonight. Still, his larger body is using up more oxygen than he can take in, meaning he's just about reached the limits of his ability. While I can push through, it won't be easy. I can find a way to manage to go until the end of this game at full speed.

Sure enough, they try to throw another high pass to Green right over top of me. Time to break out my high jumping skills. I leap into the air with all the vertical force I can gather. Green wasn't expecting me to get that high, and as a result doesn't follow me into the air. I grab the ball at the height of my jump, stealing it away and shocking the other team. The crowd cheers with a loud roar. Instantly, I chest pass the ball to Wyatt. He is able to sink a quick 3-point shot from the corner, bringing the Huxley lead down to 12.

"GET IT TOGETHER, GREEN! YOU TOWER OVER THIS KID FOR CRYING OUT LOUD!" I hear the Huxley coach yell out. I take a little pride in the fact that I am frustrating them.

We use the same tactics and keep cutting down the lead. It gets easier with each passing minute as Green wears down even more, but we are also in a race against the clock. Thankfully, we are close to an almost unheard of second half shut out. Our whole team is playing defense like never before, refusing to give up an inch. As the clock hits 41 seconds left, the score is 44 to 45. The crowd is electric, and it really feels like we're about to make history. Wyatt and AJ were able to make a 3-pointer each, and John was able to score 2 lay ups and a free throw to get us to this point. We just need a steal and two points to win it as the Huxley center looks for an open man to throw the ball in to.

This time he tries to throw it a little farther down court to their power forward, who is being guarded by Matt. Their power forward, wearing the number 33, catches the ball and begins to drive down the court. Fouling here might be smart, but if they make both free throws it will make it that much harder to win. It'll be better to just play good defense and use our 6 seconds after the shot clock runs down to try and make a fast basket.

Huxley plays a hesitant drive, moving the ball very little, seemingly placing all their bets on laying low instead of trying to increase their lead. They are successful in holding the ball until the shot clock buzzes. The Huxley coach calls a timeout at that moment, giving his players one last moment to catch their breath before the final play of the game.

"Alright, boys! One last possession! Let's go get this dub!" Matt hypes us up. "Everyone bring it in. I am going to lay out our final play." Coach Morgan tells us.

After he lays out the plan, we take the court. The stakes are high, so high in fact, that I have too much adrenaline coursing through my veins to even be nervous. I meet the gaze of Aidan Green as we step back on the court. His breath is controlled now after the break. His eyes have a certain intensity to them. There's no doubt about it, this man is a competitor. He may be wounded but his pride won't let him roll over and die. He wants this win just as bad as I do. This won't be easy.

The whistle blows and play resumes. I take off sprinting from our side of the court to the other end, Green hot on my tail. The Huxley defense looks my way to predict my quick movement. However, John doesn't pass the ball to me as the defense would expect. Instead, he passes it short to AJ. The defense is quick to react to this. While eyes are on him, I stop mid sprint and hit a comeback route, freeing me a little bit of space from Green. AJ jumps high and bullets a pass that hits me well in the hands as the clock hits 4 seconds.

Only Aidan and I stand on the Huxley side of the court. A one on one to decide the game. For as loud as the room is, in my head, it's as if Aidan and I are the only two here. My focus makes the world around me seem to vanish. I make one shifty move and bounce the ball between my legs before taking off at full speed to the right of Green. He stays with me step by step as we approach the basket. Soon, we make it to our destination, and with no time to set up a shot, I force my feet into the ground and push off. Green jumps up with me, arm above his head looking to block my dunk attempt. I jump just high enough to go for a two-handed dunk. Green throws his hand in front of the ball, but the strength of both my arms overpowers him. I push right through his force and slam the ball through the rim, grabbing the rim and hanging from it in the process.

Green falls over as a result of me jumping through him. I drop from the rim and come back to the world as the deafening noise of screaming Stag's fans fill the room. I take a large breath and look at the clock. 0.2 seconds left. Talk about a close call.

The referee gives the ball to Huxley. Who is allowed to inbound it, but there isn't even close to enough time to do anything. The game ends as soon as the ball hit their shooting guard's hands.

I look over to Green who walks over to me. I fully expect him to be angry. Instead, he extends his hand out to me. "That was a great game, man. Respect. I hope I see you again at the next level." He tells me, referring to college ball.

"Yeah. Thanks, man. I appreciate that." I say back, sincerely. Before I can continue our conversation, I am swept off my feet by a bear hug from John. He promptly puts me on his shoulders and starts to parade me around the gym as the fans chant my name. This moment is one I know I will never forget.

I see the faces of my loved ones and friends all happy for me. Pure joy invades my heart. The only words that come to my brain in seeing all this are a simple few.

'Thank you, God.'

CHAPTER 21

Banquet

"I am now going to call up the winner of our most valuable player award, John Lynn!" Coach Morgan makes his announcement to a crowded school lunchroom full of our basketball team all sitting with their respective families. This sort of thing is customary after a sports season. It's a way for the school to show thanks to all the players.

Our season is done. We played all the way to the Iowa State Championship, where we lost by a heartbreaking 5 points. The thing is no one was that heartbroken about it. We all fought to the end. When it came down to it, I think we all realized that we still accomplished something special. Even John and Matt, who wouldn't be able to get another crack at the title next year, were as happy as the rest of us about our play this year. From losing our first game ruining my whole week, to just being happy I got to play the game I enjoy, I think I learned a lot this year. Even if I still hate losing, I see it as just another obstacle to overcome, instead of an end all. Getting to enjoy the championship after missing out on the experience my sophomore year was a plus as well.

John got up from our table. He chose to sit with my mom, Shelby, and I. His father didn't decide to come tonight. A fact that I can't tell if John prefers or is secretly hurt by. Earlier in the day he explained to us that he accepted a football scholarship to a school in Nebraska. Even though we've made a friendship this year and I'll be sad he's leaving. I could not be happier for him, not only has he earned it, but the football team will have him move into a dorm at the start of summer. Just a few short months away. Giving him what I suspect is much needed space from his father.

He weaves through the lunchroom tables making his way to Coach Morgan at the front. Coach looks the part of our award host tonight. It looks as if he put on his nicest sweat suit and combed his mustache.

John gets to the front of the room and accepts his trophy. It's a fake gold statue of a man preforming a jump shot, with the letters 'MVP' engraved on the bottom. I am glad to see this award go to John. It would look good in my room, but his stats are hard to argue. Highest points, blocks, and rebounds, it is well deserved.

John wears a large smile as he eats up the attention. "Speech, Speech, Speech!" All our players begin to chant. This gets a chuckle out of Coach as he hands the mic to John.

"Alright, Alright." John says sarcastically, rolling his eyes, akin to if he were pleasing the paparazzi with a photo. "First off, I want to say it's been an honor to play here the last four years for Coach Morgan." Applause results from that statement. "Second, I would like to thank my teammates. A lot of my points came from assists from our guards. Without good play from our forwards, I never would have been freed up enough to do much of anything. This team as a whole has earned a trophy. That said... I will gladly accept this one, thank you all!"

Laughs and clapping come from the team and their families as John concludes his speech.

We all share a meal together, one that will probably be our last. Who knows if the members of this year's team will ever all be together again without our sport holding us together. Only time will tell.

Soon, everyone finishes their meals. One by one, people make their exit, including John, Matt, and AJ. "Alright, Rick. I'll see you back home. You too have fun tonight." My mom says to Shelby and I before seeing her way out of the school.

Yes, we did go on that date we talked about, and it went really well. Our conversation went so smoothly, I lost track of time and ended up missing my curfew. All is well that ends well though, and I landed myself another date tonight.

We decide it's time to head out as well and make a path toward the school entrance. Just after walking out of the door, I see Wyatt and Ava saying goodbye to Wyatt's family, as they must be going on a date after the banquet as well. "Hey Shelby, I think I am going to tell Wyatt goodbye before we take off." I say.

"Sure thing, I'll go start the car." She says back politely. Before she turns to walk to her car, she unexpectedly plants a kiss on me. She smiles before walking away leaving me with a dumbfounded grin in her wake. Then, I practically float over to Wyatt and Ava, who are alone now.

My two best friends. The ones who helped me through the most difficult year of my life. I don't know what our future as friends holds, if we'll always be as close as we are now, or if time will take its toll on our relationship. One thing I do know is those two will never really know how much they mean to me.

"Hey, bro!" Wyatt greets me. Instead of saying anything back, I pull him in for a hug. He lets out a "Guh!" as he was caught off guard by my squeeze.

"Hey now, should I be jealous?" Ava jokes just before I reach out my arm pulling her into our hug as well. The two are confused and gasping for air with the intensity I squeeze them.

"I love you guys…" I tell them.

They share a look before Wyatt responds. "Yeah, we love you too, buddy."

"You guys don't know how much I needed you this year... and you came through. Bro, if you never got me out of the house, I think I would have just stayed in my room gaming all year."

"Yeah... I did know how much you needed me. you went through something incredibly hard. I wouldn't have deserved the right to be called your best friend if I didn't drop everything until I knew you were okay."

"Well, rest assured, you are my best friend. You know I would do the same for you?"

"Of course, man."

And with that, I release my grip on them. I tell them my goodbyes for the night, and head off to meet Shelby.

EPILOGUE

ALMOST FIVE YEARS LATER:

"I'll be darned! Rick Joseph! How the heck are you?" Mr. Hugh greets me in the church parking lot while gripping my hand with the strength of a silverback.

"I've been good, man! How are you?" I ask, pulling my aching hand back to my side. It's a nice summer day. The weather is perfect as one by one Mr. Hugh's students start to arrive.

"Doing great! I am so glad you had time to pop in and share your story with my class tonight. Former Iowa State Champ, and now player at Iowa State, that's the sort of thing these kids look up to." Mr. Hugh tells me. That's right, we ended up pulling it off and brought home a State Championship for the Stags my senior year of high school. Now here I am, about to go into my senior year of college, and the way things are looking, I am finally going to start at the D1 level.

"Yeah, of course. I am happy to help however I can."

"Oh, and how has Shelby been? You two are still together, right?"

"Oh yeah. She's great. She wanted to make it tonight but her team is traveling this week."

"Not to worry, I am just thrilled to hear you both are doing so well. Your mom brags about you both every time I see her at Sunday service."

Before I can respond a small bus pulls up, letting out about 8 teenage boys. "These are the boys from a new program the church started. We bus around local kids in the system, most of which have been in and out of foster care for some time." Mr. Hugh tells me. One boy in particular doesn't follow the group, he instead goes and sits on the curb near the outdoor basketball hoop the church had set up.

"All these boys have had a rough go, some more than others. That one there, his name is Chance… and I have had a hard time getting through to him. He has been in foster care in different homes for as long as he can remember. He's never had any real parental guidance."

The boy sits there, looking as if defeated is the state in which he lives his whole life. This can't help but remind me of the way I felt when I was at my lowest. "Do you mind if I talk to him?" I ask. Mr. Hugh gives me a nod and I walk over to the boy, not really knowing what I will say when I get there. Will I start with a cheesy 'I know how you feel'? or will I try and make awkward small talk before diving in. I step closer and make my approach.

"What do you want?" Chance asks me. The sun glares in my eyes off of the back board of the nearby hoop. The ray of light hits me with an idea. I remember the hoop in my driveway. That was the only way Wyatt was able to get me out of my room. Soon enough, I was able to open up and let my guard down through the fun I had playing. It seems like it's maybe all coming full circle.

"I got a ball in my car. How about a game?" I say, looking at Chance and then back at the hoop. Chance looks at me surprised. He is probably used to everyone trying to help him, but not as much someone just wanting to spend time with him. After a moment, the boy, probably only 13 or 14 years old, lets out a smile. "Alright, yeah. You're on!"

END

www.ingramcontent.com/pod-product-compliance
Lightning Source LLC
Chambersburg PA
CBHW071123090426
42736CB00012B/1991